Eyewitness
VIKING

Part of a gilded bronze
harness from Broa, Sweden

Two gold rings

Sword
handle from
Denmark,
ninth centu

Amber game piece
from Denmark

Resurrection egg

Gold arm-ring
from Denmark

Viking peasant warrior

10th-century figure of m
riding horse, Swe

Eyewitness
VIKING

lica of a ship's
achable figurehead

Gilded bronze
harness bow
from Denmark

Written by
SUSAN M. MARGESON

Photographed by
PETER ANDERSON

Belt mount from the
Volga region in Russia

Thor's hammer

Norwegian
Urnes-style brooch

DK
DK Publishing, Inc.

The Åby Crucifix,
Denmark, c. 1100

Animal-head post from
the Oseberg ship-burial,
Norway, c. 800–850

DK

LONDON, NEW YORK, MUNICH,
MELBOURNE, and DELHI

Project editor Scott Steedman
Art editor Andrew Nash
Managing editor Simon Adams
Managing art editor Julia Harris
Researcher Céline Carez
Production Catherine Semark
Picture research Julia Ruxton
Editorial consultant David M. Wilson

REVISED EDITION
Managing editor Andrew Macintyre
Managing art editor Jane Thomas
Editor and reference compiler Lorrie Mack
Art editor Rebecca Johns
Production Jenny Jacoby
Picture research Brenda Clynch
DTP designer Siu Yin Ho

U.S. editors Elizabeth Hester, John Searcy
Publishing director Beth Sutinis
Art director Dirk Kaufman
U.S. DTP designer Milos Orlovic
U.S. production Chris Avgherinos, Ivor Parker

This Eyewitness ® Guide has been conceived by
Dorling Kindersley Limited and Editions Gallimard

This edition published in the United States in 2005
by DK Publishing, Inc.
375 Hudson Street, New York, NY 10014

04 05 06 07 08 09 10 9 8 7 6 5 4 3 2 1

A catalog record for this book is
available from the Library of Congress.

ISBN 0-7566-1095-8 (Hardcover) 0-7566-1096-6 (Library Binding)

Color reproduction by
Colourscan, Singapore
Printed in China by Toppan Printing Co.,
(Shenzhen) Ltd.

Discover more at
www.dk.com

Silver brooch
from Birka,
Sweden

Danish
coins

Bronze key from
Gotland, Sweden

Silver pendant of
a Viking woman

Gilded bronze mount from
horse's bridle, Broa, Sweden

The Jelling Cup

Contents

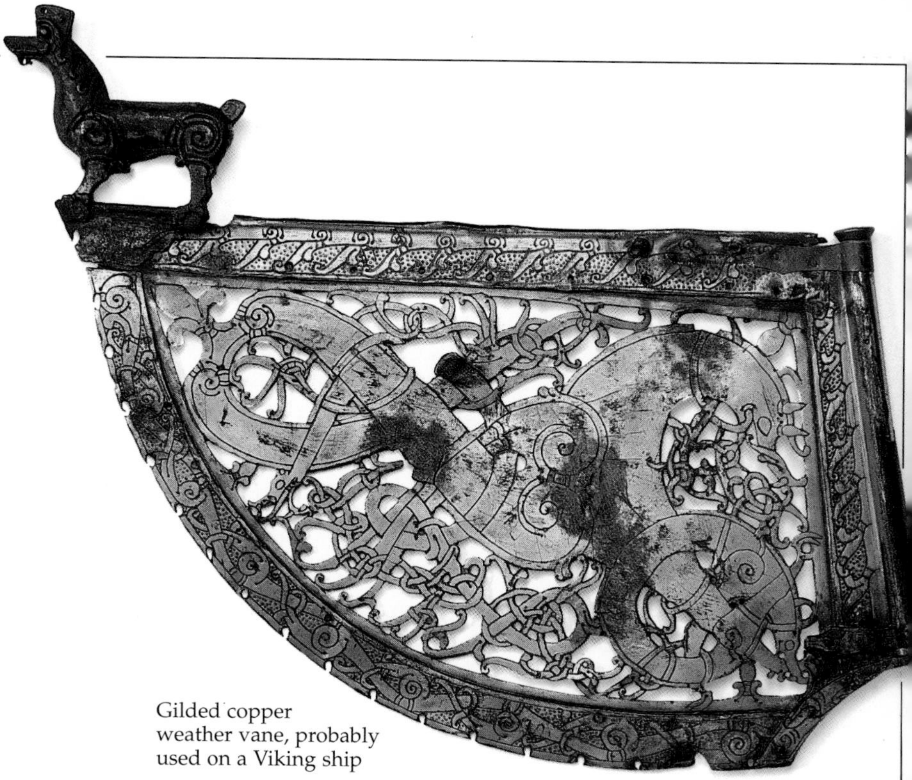

Gilded copper
weather vane, probably
used on a Viking ship

Who were the Vikings?

For 300 years, from the 8th to 11th centuries, the Vikings took the world by storm. In search of land, slaves, gold, and silver, these brave warriors and explorers set sail from their homes in Norway, Sweden, and Denmark. They raided all across Europe, voyaged as far as Baghdad, and even reached America. The speed and daring of Viking attacks became legendary. Christian monks wrote with horror about the violent raids on rich monasteries and towns. But the Vikings were more than wild barbarians from the north. They were shrewd traders, excellent navigators, and superb craftsmen and shipbuilders.They had a rich tradition of story-telling, and lived in a society that was open and democratic for its day.

ROMANTIC VIKINGS
There are many romantic legends about Vikings. Most of them are wrong! Many pictures show them wearing horned helmets. But real Vikings wore round or pointed caps of iron or leather (p. 13).

CATTY BROOCH
A Swedish Viking held his cloak in place with this brooch. It is made of silver coated in gold. The details are highlighted with niello, a black substance like enamel. The style of decoration, with little catlike heads, is known as the Borre style.

SCARY SHIP
Vikings often carved terrifying beasts on their ships to scare their enemies (p. 10). This dragon head was found in a river bed in Holland. It dates from the 5th century, 300 years before the Viking Age. It may have been part of a Saxon warship sunk during a raid. Sailing ships were known before the Vikings, but they were less sophisticated. Viking ships were fast and flexible, and could cruise up narrow channels and inlets with ease.

THE VIKING WORLD
The brown areas on this map are Viking lands and colonies. From late in the 8th century, Vikings raided, traded, and explored far and wide. They discovered Iceland in 870, and sailed further west to Greenland in 985 (pp. 20–21). Leif the Lucky was probably the first European to set foot on America. He is thought to have landed in Newfoundland, Canada, in 1001. In the East, Vikings sailed the Baltic Sea and continued up rivers into Russia. They went overland as far as Constantinople (now Istanbul) and Jerusalem. Vikings also sailed around the west coast of Europe and into the Mediterranean Sea. Thanks to their fast ships and skill at seafaring, they could take people completely by surprise.

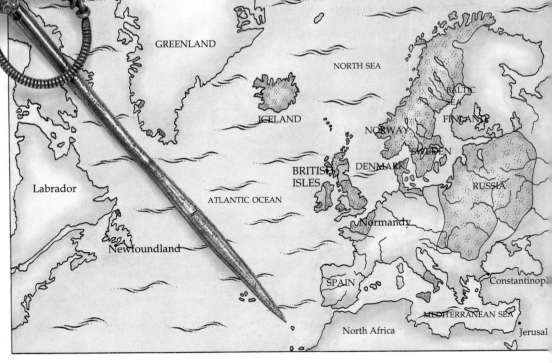

...ver wires in
...form of plant
...ots

...E OF
...HIEFTAIN
...s great iron
...head was found in
...mmen, Denmark. It is
...orated with silver wires.
...s side features a glaring human
...e and a fantastic bird that twists
...und its own wings, which turn into plant
...ots. The Mammen Axe is too beautiful to have
...n used in battle, and must have been carried by
...hieftain to show his power.

*Silver loop
for chain*

*Figure of
great bird*

GLITTERING SWORD
A strong sword was a
Viking's most prized
weapon (pp. 14–15).
This sword was made
and decorated in Norway.
Its owner must have died at
battle in Ireland, because it was
found in a man's grave in Dublin.
It is beautifully crafted. The hilt
and guard are made of copper
decorated with layers of gold and
twisted silver and copper wires.

Pommel

*Grip,
once
covered
in
leather*

*Guard to
protect hand*

*Helmet with
bird's crest
and beak*

*Loop so hammer
could be worn on
chain around neck*

THOR'S HAMMER
Vikings believed in
many different gods
(pp. 52–53). This silver
hammer is the sign of the
great god Thor. He was said
to ride his chariot across
the sky, smashing
giant snakes with his
hammer and making
thunder and lightning.

Mustache

MYSTERIOUS
VIKING FACE
Who is this
Viking? A god? A
hero from a legend?
A warrior? Real pictures
of Vikings are very rare.
The Vikings didn't have
books, and most of the people and
animals (pp. 36–37) in their art are
imaginary or hard to identify. This
small silver head from Aska, Sweden,
was worn on a chain as a pendant.
It may have been meant to ward
off enemies or bring good luck.

Mouth

HERE COME
THE VIKINGS!
Ivar the Boneless and
his army invaded England
in 869. This English manuscript
(made 300 years later) shows
Ivar's warships arriving at the
coast. The first raiders are
walking down gangplanks onto
the shore. Ivar and his men
terrorized the country and
killed King Edmund (p. 17).

Iron blade, now rusted

Lords of the sea

THE VIKINGS WERE SUPERB sailors. Their wooden ships carried them across wild seas, riding the waves, dodging rocks and icebergs. In open seas, the Vikings relied on the ships' big, rectangular sail and navigated by the sun and stars. Their knowledge of seabirds, fish, winds, and wave patterns also helped them find their way. But whenever possible, they sailed within sight of land. To maneuver in coastal waters and rivers, they dropped the mast and rowed the ship instead. Wood rots quickly, so there is little left of most ships. But fortunately a few have survived, thanks to the Viking custom of burying rich people in ships (pp. 54–57). The best preserved are the Oseberg and Gokstad ships from Norway. Both are slender, elegant vessels, light but surprisingly strong.

Stem-post or prow

Ship is made of light oak wood with heavier mast of pine

DIGGING OUT THE SHIP
The Norwegian ships were preserved by unusual wet condition[s]. The Gokstad ship sat in a large mound and had a burial chambe[r] on its deck. A man's skeleton lay in the chamber, surrounded by his worldly possessions. He had been buried around 900 A.D.

SAILING TO THE WINDY CITY
The Gokstad ship had 32 shields on each side, painted yellow and black alternately. A full-size replica was sailed across the Atlantic Ocean to Newfoundland and then to Chicago in 1893. It proved how seaworthy the real ship must have been.

Gunwale (top strake)

Sixteen strakes (planks) on each side, each one overlapping the strake below

LEARNING THE ROPES
Coins and picture stones give clues about how Viking ships were rigged (roped) and sailed. This coin from Birka, Sweden shows a ship with a furle[d] (rolled-up) sail.

Sixteen oar-ports (holes) on each side

GOKSTAD SHIP, FRONT VIEW
One of the grandest Viking ships was found at Gokstad, beside Oslo Fjord (inlet) in Norway. It was excavated in 1880. The elegant lines of the prow and strakes (planks) show the skill of the ship-builders. The ship is 76 ft (23.2 m) long and 17 ft (5.2 m) wide. The keel is a single piece of oak, cut from a tree at least 82 ft (25 m) tall!

Keel

RAISING THE GOKSTAD MAST
The heavy mast was lowered into a groove in the keelson and held in place by the mast fish. The deck boards were loose, so the sailors could store their belongings under them.

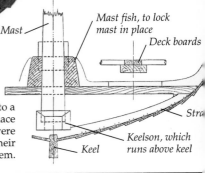

Mast

Mast fish, to lock mast in place

Deck boards

Stra[ke]

Keelson, which runs above keel

Keel

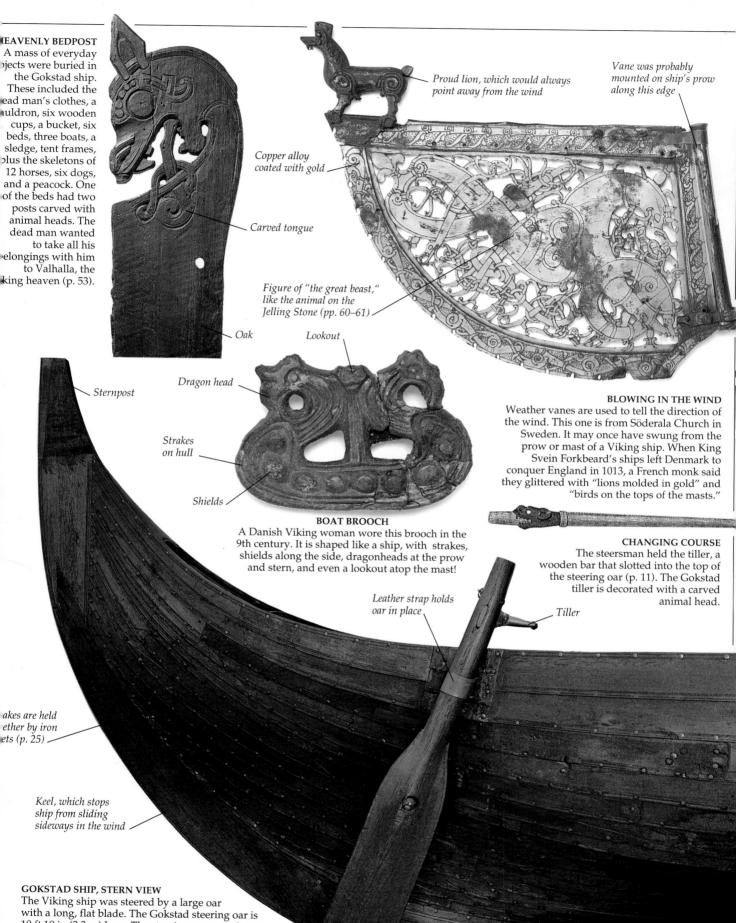

EAVENLY BEDPOST
A mass of everyday
objects were buried in
the Gokstad ship.
These included the
dead man's clothes, a
cauldron, six wooden
cups, a bucket, six
beds, three boats, a
sledge, tent frames,
plus the skeletons of
12 horses, six dogs,
and a peacock. One
of the beds had two
posts carved with
animal heads. The
dead man wanted
to take all his
belongings with him
to Valhalla, the
viking heaven (p. 53).

Carved tongue

Oak

Sternpost

Proud lion, which would always
point away from the wind

Vane was probably
mounted on ship's prow
along this edge

Copper alloy
coated with gold

Figure of "the great beast,"
like the animal on the
Jelling Stone (pp. 60–61)

Lookout

Dragon head

Strakes
on hull

Shields

BLOWING IN THE WIND
Weather vanes are used to tell the direction of
the wind. This one is from Söderala Church in
Sweden. It may once have swung from the
prow or mast of a Viking ship. When King
Svein Forkbeard's ships left Denmark to
conquer England in 1013, a French monk said
they glittered with "lions molded in gold" and
"birds on the tops of the masts."

BOAT BROOCH
A Danish Viking woman wore this brooch in the
9th century. It is shaped like a ship, with strakes,
shields along the side, dragonheads at the prow
and stern, and even a lookout atop the mast!

CHANGING COURSE
The steersman held the tiller, a
wooden bar that slotted into the top of
the steering oar (p. 11). The Gokstad
tiller is decorated with a carved
animal head.

Leather strap holds
oar in place

Tiller

akes are held
ether by iron
ets (p. 25)

Keel, which stops
ship from sliding
sideways in the wind

GOKSTAD SHIP, STERN VIEW
The Viking ship was steered by a large oar
with a long, flat blade. The Gokstad steering oar is
10 ft 10 in (3.3 m) long. The steering oar was always
attached to the right side of the ship near the stern, or
back. A ship's right side is still called starboard, after
the old Norse word *styra* (to steer). The Gokstad ship
is symmetrical – the prow, or front, is identical to the
stern, except that it has no steering oar.

Steering oar

A Viking warship

T HE VIKING WARSHIP was the longest, slenderest, and quickest of Viking vessels, and carried warriors far across the ocean. Like oth Viking ships, the warship had a sail and mast, but it could also be rowed. Depending on its size, a warship would have 24 to 50 oars and carry at least as many warriors. On long voyages, the Viking warriors rowed in shifts. They could glide their ship up narrow inlets and land on any flat beach. Even when it was full, the warship had such a shallow keel that it did not need a landing jet and could be unloaded right on the shore. Some warships like the ships on the Bayeux Tapestry (below) could carry horses a well as warriors. When beached, both animals and men would wade ashore. Two well-preserved warships were discovered in the Roskilde Fjord in Denmark. They had been filled with stones and deliberately sunk around the year 1000. One is 92 ft (28 m) from prow to stern the longest Viking ship ever found.

UNWELCOME GUESTS
A ship full of fierce warriors suddenly landing on the beach filled people with fear and horror. This highly romanticized picture of raiders appeared in a French magazine in 1911.

Dragon made of carved and painted pine wood

Detachable wooden figurehead

DANISH DRAGON SHIP
In 1962, five Viking ships were excavated from Roskilde Fjord in Sjælland, Denmark. They had been scuttled (sunk deliberately), probably to block a channel and protect the harbor from enemy ships. This is a reconstruction of one of the warships. It was 57 ft (17.4 m) long and only 8 ft 6 in (2.6 m) across at the widest point. The ship had seven strakes (planks) on each side, the top three made of ash, the bottom four of oak. There were 12 oar-ports (holes) on each side, so 24 men could row together.

Leather thong holds figurehead in place

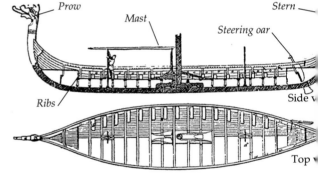

Prow   Mast   Stern

Steering oar

Ribs   Side v

Top

A SHIP AND A HALF
Cross beams and ribs helped to strengthen the hull of a Viking ship. The gaps between the strakes were stuffed with tarred wool. This is called caulking. It kept the water out, and made the ship more flexible in rough seas.

Original rope may have been made of walrus skin   *Mooring*

Hull made of seven slender strakes

WILLIAM'S WARSHIP
The Normans were descended from Vikings who settled in Normandy, France. The Bayeux Tapestry, embroidered in the 11th century, describes their conquest of England in 1066. Here the proud ship of the Norman leader William the Conqueror sails toward England. A lookout in the stern blows a horn, while the steersman holds the tiller, attached to the steering oar. The ship has an animal-head prow, and shields line its sides.

Each strake overlaps the one below, in a technique called "clinker" boat-building

FOR THE TILLERMAN
At right is a modern replica of a tiller. It slotted into a hole at the top of the steering oar. The steersman always held the tiller level. By moving it to fore (forward) or aft (backward), he turned the ship to the left or right. The rope would have been tied to a peg in the deck, to stop the tiller from swinging wildly in a storm.

Slot for tiller

Rope made of plant fiber such as hemp

Carved and painted wood

Rigging, the ship's ropes

Sail made of wool or linen, sometimes quilted in stripes or diamond pattern

Stern (back)

Steering oar

Prow (front)

Lower slot for attaching oar to gunwale

In Viking times, this rope would have been made of willow or pine

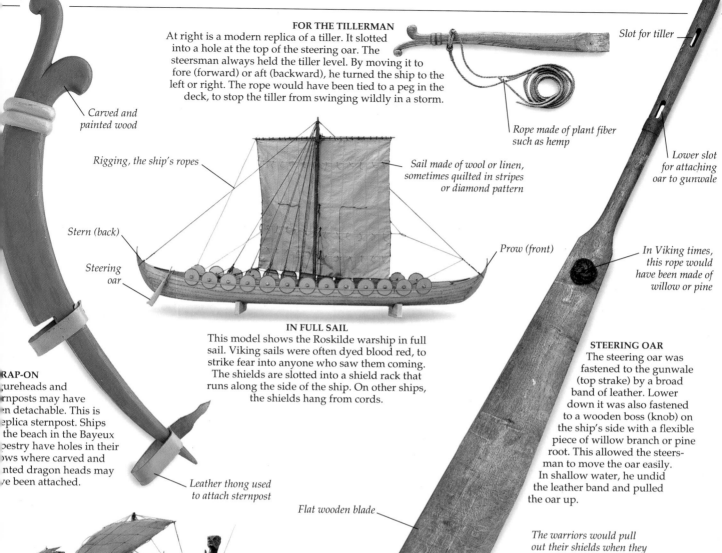

IN FULL SAIL
This model shows the Roskilde warship in full sail. Viking sails were often dyed blood red, to strike fear into anyone who saw them coming. The shields are slotted into a shield rack that runs along the side of the ship. On other ships, the shields hang from cords.

STEERING OAR
The steering oar was fastened to the gunwale (top strake) by a broad band of leather. Lower down it was also fastened to a wooden boss (knob) on the ship's side with a flexible piece of willow branch or pine root. This allowed the steersman to move the oar easily. In shallow water, he undid the leather band and pulled the oar up.

RAP-ON
…ureheads and …rnposts may have …n detachable. This is …eplica sternpost. Ships … the beach in the Bayeux …pestry have holes in their …ws where carved and …nted dragon heads may …e been attached.

Leather thong used to attach sternpost

Flat wooden blade

The warriors would pull out their shields when they fought at sea or landed on a foreign beach

RUNNING WITH THE WIND
These warships are loosely based on the ships …und at Gokstad and Oseberg in Norway. With a …od wind behind it, a Viking warship was fast. In …3, the replica of the Gokstad ship took 28 days to sail from Sweden to Newfoundland, Canada.

Shield rack, a long plank behind which the shields could be rested

Gunwale (top strake)

Viking warriors

THE TRUE SPIRIT OF THE VIKING AGE was daring courage. To the Viking warrior, honor and glory in battle were the only things that lasted forever. A warrior had to be ready to follow his lord or king into battle or on a raid or expedition. As a member of a loyal band of followers, known as a *lið*, he could be called up to fight at any moment. In the later Viking Age, kings had the power to raise a force (or *leiðang*) of ships, men, supplies, and weapons. The kingdom was divided into small units, each unit providing one warrior. Groups of units donated a ship to carry the warriors on a raid to faraway lands.

ARCHER IN ACTION

Vikings were skilled with bow and arrow, both in battle and hunting. A well-preserved bow was found in Hedeby, the great Danish Viking town, now in Germany. It was made of yew wood. A rich boat buri in Hedeby contained bundle of arrows wit bronze mounts. The probably belonged to a nobleman.

Bow made of flexible wood such as yew

Fur hat

Shaft of flexible birch wood

Sharp iron arrowhead

Flights, pieces of feathers added to stabilize arrow in air

Bear-tooth pendant

Bowstring of twisted fibers

Bundle of arrows

Leather sheath for knife

Leather quiver, a pouch for holding arrows

Round shield

Sw

Conical helmet

Spear

BOUND FOR GLORY

In this romantic engraving, warriors fight with axe and sword. The Viking poem *Hávamál* says:
"Cattle die,
kindred die,
every man is mortal:
but I know one thing
that never dies,
The glory of the
great dead."

STONE WARRIOR

This Viking warrior was carved in the 10th century on a stone cross in Middleton, Yorkshire, England. His weapons are laid out around him as they would have been in a traditional burial (pp. 54–57). The Anglo-Saxon poem *The Battle of Maldon* describes the noise and fury of a battle between Danish Vikings and the English: "Then they let the spears, hard as a file, go from their hands; let the darts [arrows], ground sharp, fly; bows were busy; shield received point; bitter was the rush of battle."

Axe

THE LATEST FASHION
Vikings usually fought on foot. However, in the late 11th century, at the end of the Viking Age, cavalry began to be used in battle. This mounted warrior is from a tapestry woven in Baldishol, Norway, around the year 1200. He is wearing a helmet and chain-mail tunic, and carrying a kite-shaped shield. These longer shields protected the body better than round ones.

Iron spearhead

Iron plates welded together

Chain mail may have hung at the back to protect neck

REAL HELMET (NO HORNS)
The typical Viking helmet was shaped like this one from Gjermundbu in Norway. It has "goggles" to protect the eyes.

Iron helmet with noseguard

Wooden shaft

Chain mail to protect neck

Brooch

Padded leather tunic

Baldric, a strap used to carry a sword

ONE HEAVY SHIRT
These fragments of a chain-mail shirt come from Gjermundbu, Norway. Making chain mail was a slow job. Each iron ring had to be forged separately. Then it was linked to the last one and closed with a rivet or welded in place. It took thousands of rings to make one shirt.

Sword guard to protect hand

Chain-mail tunic, long enough to cover waist

ᏟUAL DRESS
ᏟᎥke Roman legionaries ᏟᏁodern soldiers, ᏟᎥng warriors didn't ᏟᏒ uniforms. Every ᏟᎥer had to dress and ᏟᎵ himself. Chieftains ᏟᎥron helmets and ᏟᎥ. Poor warriors had to ᏟᏁke do with leather ᏟᎥing, which didn't ᏟᎥ as much protection ᏟᎥain mail. Leather ᏟᏟs were worn instead, ᏟᎥ leather caps were ᏟᎥ common than iron ᏟᎥets. Shields of wood ᏟᎥ iron were a Viking's ᏟᎥ defense against ᏟᎥs and blows from ᏟᎥ swords.

Iron sword

Tweed trousers

Wooden shield with iron boss (stud)

Sheath for sword

Men probably wore woolen socks, like one found in York, England

Leather shoes, often made of goat skin

Weapons

His spear, his axe, his shield, and especially his sword – these were a warrior's most prized possessions. In poems and sagas (pp. 52–53), swords were given names celebrating the strength and sharpness of the blade or the glittering decoration of the hilt (handle). Weapons were made of iron, and often decorated with inlaid or encrusted silver or copper. A beautifully ornamented sword was a sign that the owner was rich or powerful. Before the arrival of Christianity, a Viking's weapons were usually buried with him when he died. Helmets (p. 13) are rarely found, because most of them were made of leather and have rotted away.

Notch to cut feathers

Broad iron blade

Wooden board about 3 ft (1 m) in diameter

Leather binding to protect the edges

ARROWS
Arrows were used for hunting as well as for battle (p. 12). These iron arrowheads from Norway would have been lashed to shafts of birch wood. The two on the right were used to hunt reindeer. The other one was designed for killing birds.

THRUSTING AND THROWING
Spears were mainly used as thrusting weapons, and had large broad blades. The sockets were often decorated. Throwing spears had much lighter, narrower blades, so they would fly straight and true.

Geometric patterns of copper and silver

Wooden shaft was riveted into socket

BERSERK
Tyr was the Viking god of war. In this romantic engraving he has a shaggy bearskin cloak, with the bear's head worn as a helmet. Wa called *berserkir* prepared for battle by putting on bearskin or shirts and working themselves into a frenzy. This was c going *berserk*, from the Old Norse word meaning "bear sh

Iron thrusting spearhead from
Ronnesbæksholm, Sjælland, Denmark

Iron throwing spearhead from
Fyrkat fortress, Jutland, Denmark

SHIELD

Viking shields were round and made of wood. Unfortunately, wood rots quickly, and very few shields have survived. This one is a replica based on fragments found with the Roskilde warship (pp. 10–11). The iron boss in the center protected the warrior's hand holding the shield by a grip on the other side of the boss. Shields were often covered in leather or painted in bright colors. A Viking poem, *Ragnarsdrápa*, describes a shield painted with pictures of gods and heroes.

Geometric patterns of inlaid silver

Decorative knob

AXES

Axes with long wooden handles were the most common Viking weapon. T-shaped axes were usually used for working wood (p. 45). But the example above is so richly decorated that it must have been a weapon – and a sign of prestige or power.

Iron rivets

Hole for wooden handle, which has rotted away

Rounded pommel

Broad iron blade

Iron axehead from Fyrkat, Denmark

Iron axehead from Trelleborg, Denmark

DOUBLE-EDGED SWORDS

Swords were usually double-edged. The blacksmith (pp. 44–45) sometimes pattern-welded the blades for extra strength. He did this by fusing several strips of iron together. Then he twisted the metal, hammered it out, and polished it smooth. By adding carbon to the iron while it was red-hot, he produced sharp steel edges. Hilts and pommels were often highly decorated.

ble-edged
rd from
nsholm,
dersø,
mark

t decorated
h geometric
terns of
er and
ss

CHAIN GANG

In this detail from the Bayeux Tapestry (p. 10), Norman warriors carry weapons and chain-mail suits to their ships. The suits of mail (p. 13) are so heavy that each one is carried on a pole between two men. This also stops the chain-mail from getting tangled up. Viking weapons would have been similar.

Pattern-welded iron blade

Straight sword guard

Grip

Pommel

Iron sword from Denmark

Fuller, a central groove that makes the sword lighter and more flexible

Terrorizing the West

T HE VIKINGS SWEPT into western Europe, terrorizing towns along the coast, plundering churches, and grabbing riches, slaves, and land. The first recorded raid, on the famous monastery of Lindisfarne in 793, shocked the whole Christian world. From then on, attacks all over Europe intensified. Bands of Viking warriors roamed the North Sea and the English Channel, raiding choice targets at will. Soon the Vikings were venturing further inland. They sailed up the great rivers Europe – the Rhine, Seine, Rhone, and Loire – and even overran Paris. The raiders began to spend winters in areas they had captured. Then they up bases to attack other targets. The Vikings o demanded huge payments for leaving an area peace. Some warriors were off raiding for year Björn Jarnsmiða and his companion Hasting spent three years with 62 ships in Spain, North Africa, France, and Italy. They lost a lot of thei treasure in storms on the way home.

Lead weight w
animal head m
in Ireland

THROWN INTO THE THAMES
This Viking sword was found in the River Thames in London. This big English city was attacked many times, once by 94 ships. But it was never taken.

SOUVENIR OF PARIS
Paris was conquered on Easter Sunday, March 28, 845. Charles the Bald, the French king, had to pay the raiders 7,000 lb (3,175 kg) of silver to get peace. The Viking leader Ragnar even took a bar from the city gate as a souvenir. But he and most of his men died of disease on their way back to Scandinavia.

Rusted iron blade

HOLY SLAUGHTER
Lindisfarne is a small island off the east coast of England. The celebrated monastery there was destroyed by Vikings in 793. These warriors on a stone from the island may well be the Viking raiders. The *Anglo-Saxon Chronicle*, a contemporary English historical record, reported: "the ravages of heathen men miserably destroyed God's church on Lindisfarne, with plunder and slaughter."

RAIDING FRANCE
This picture of a Viking ship is in a French manuscript from around 1100. Viking ships attacked French towns and monasteries all through the 9th century. One group of Vikings settled in the Seine region. Another band under the chieftain Rollo made their homes around Rouen. This area became known as Normandy, "Land of the Northmen" (p. 10).

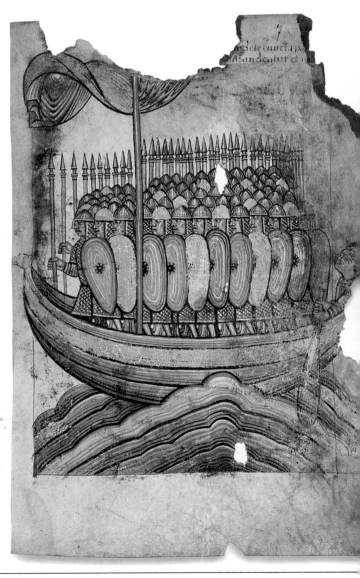

KILLING THE KING

King Edmund was king of East Anglia in England in 869. This 12th-century manuscript shows him being beaten by Vikings. Then they tied him to a tree and shot him full of arrows. He still refused to give up his belief in Christ, so they cut his head off. The Vikings later settled in East Anglia under their leader King Guthrum.

Interlace designs, typical of Dublin Viking art

IRISH CROOK

Raids on Ireland began in 795. By the 820s the Vikings had worked their way around the entire island. The town of Dublin became a thriving Viking trading center with links to many other countries. This wooden animal head comes from a crook or walking stick. It was made in Dublin early in the 11th century.

SCOTCHED

This is a painting of the Viking invasion of Scotland. Many of the raiders were Norwegians who came via the Shetland and Orkney Islands. From these resting places, the many Hebridean islands, the Isle of Man (pp. 37, 51), and Ireland were all within easy reach.

Hollow box of yew wood covered in plates of tin and copper mixed with other metals

Small pieces of red enamel

Whole casket is shaped like a house

TH OF THE ARCHBISHOP

011 Archbishop Alphege of terbury was seized by Vikings were raiding the English ntryside. They were angry use the English King Ethelred n't paid them fast enough. The bishop refused to be ransomed. Vikings, who were very drunk, ed him with bones and the skulls ttle. He was finally killed with ttle-axe.

RANVAIK'S SHRINE

This shrine or casket was made in Scotland or Ireland in the 8th century. It holds holy Christian relics. It was probably taken to Norway as loot. There the new owner inscribed a message in runes (pp. 58–59) on the bottom: "Ranvaik owns this casket."

East into Russia

To cross into Russia, Viking warriors and traders sailed up various rivers such as the Dvina, Lovat, and Vistula in Poland. Then they had to drag their boats across land before they reached the headwaters of the Dniepr, Dniester, and Volga rivers and followed them south to the Black and Caspian Seas. From there, the great cities of Constantinople (heart of the Byzantine empire) and Baghdad (capital of the Islamic Caliphate) were within reach. The history of Viking raids in the East is not as well recorded as in Western Europe. But throughout Russia, Vikings left brooches, weapons, and runic inscriptions as traces of their travels. Traders swapped Siberian furs for silk, spices, and Arab silver. Vikings were even hired as Imperial guards in Constantinople.

VIKING GRAFFITI
This stone lion once stood in the Greek port of Piraeus. A Viking traveler inscribed it with long looping bands of runes, the Scandinavian writing (pp. 58–59). Much later, in 1687, Venetian soldiers carried the lion off to Venice. The runes have eroded too much to be read today. Still, such "graffiti" is often the only evidence of where Vikings traveled.

TREE OF LIFE
An Oriental tree of life is etched on the surface of this silver locket. It may have been an amulet, perhaps full of strong-smelling spices. The locket was found in a grave in Birka, Sweden. But it was probably made in the Volga area of Russia, or even as far south as Baghdad.

Silver loop for chain

EASTERN FASHIONS
Gotland is an island in the Baltic Sea. Gotland Vikings traveled far into Russia, and their excellent craftsmen often adopted styles from the East. These beads and pendant are made of rock crystal set in silver. They were probably made in Gotland, where they were found. But the style is distinctly Slav or Russian.

High-quality rock crystal shaped like a convex lens

CHECKERED PAST
This silver cup was made in the Byzantine Empire in the 11th century. It was taken back to Gotland by Vikings, who added a name and a magical inscription on the bottom in runes. The cup was buried around 1361, and found by ditch-diggers in 1881.

SWEDISH VIKINGS
Most of the Vikings who traveled to Russia and the East were Swedish. Of more than 85,000 Arabic coins found in Scandinavia, 80,000 were found in Sweden. Many 11th-century Swedish rune stones tell of voyages to the south and east. They record the deaths of travelers in Russia, Greece, the Byzantine Empire, and even Muslim lands. Most Viking settlements were temporary trading stations. Others, like Kiev and Novgorod, were more permanent. A sign of this is that women lived there too.

Birds, leaves, and winged lions

Fur hat

*nting axe with
g wooden handle*

*knife in
her sheath*

*len tunic with
roidered border*

*ggy
users in
stern
hion*

*ee-high
her boots*

GOING OVERLAND
The Russian rivers were rocky and full of rapids. The Vikings dragged or carried their light boats around these dangers. Not everyone made it. Swedish memorial stones record the deaths of many travelers in Russia and lands beyond.

A WELL-ARMED RUS
In the East, Vikings were called "Rus" by the local people. This may be where the word *Russia* comes from. Arab writers describe Viking traders armed with swords and carrying furs of black fox and beaver. The Arab Ibn Fadhlan (pp. 47, 55) said the Rus he met in 922 were "the filthiest of God's creatures." He noted with disgust that they all washed in the same bowl of water, rinsing their hair, blowing their noses, and spitting in it before passing it on to someone else!

Wooden shield

Sword

A VIKING BUDDHA?
Made in northern India in the 6th or 7th century, this bronze Buddha found its way to the Viking trading center of Helgö in Sweden. It probably stood in someone's house as a treasure.

SONG OF THE VOLGA
This is *Song of the Volga* by the Russian painter Wassili Kandinsky (1866–1944). The Volga River flows across Russia all the way to the Caspian Sea. Viking traders sailed up it in ships heavy with Arab silver. They had to pay taxes to the Russian tribespeople who lived along its banks.

Discovering new lands

THE VIKINGS WERE DARING EXPLORERS. In search of new land, they sailed their slender ships into the frozen, uncharted waters of the North Atlantic. Most of the explorers came from Norway, where the valleys were crowded and farmland was scarce. They discovered the Faroe Islands, Iceland, far-off Greenland, and "Vinland" (America). As reports of these exciting discoveries got back to Scandinavia, ships full of eager settlers set sail. Between 870 and 930, for example, more than 10,000 Vikings arrived in Iceland. They found empty spaces, wild forests, and seas teeming with fish. The sea voyages were long and dangerous, and many ships were lost in storms. But the urge to travel to new lands never dimmed.

RED AND GREEN LAND
A man called Gunnbjörn found Greenland after his ship was blown off course in a storm. The huge island was explored in 984 and 985 by Erik the Red, a chief who had been accused of murder and forced to leave Iceland. Erik encouraged hundreds of Icelanders to settle in Greenland.

THE THINGVELLIR
Iceland is a volcanic island. This high plain surrounded by great cliffs of lava was chosen as the site for the Althing, the governing assembly, which met once a year in the open air (p. 29). It is thought to have first met in 930.

Iceland

Iceland was discovered in 870. In good weather it took seven days to get there from Norway. The first settler was Ingolf, from Sunnfjord, Norway. He built a large farm on a bay overlooking the sea. This later became the capital, Reykjavik. The settlers raised sheep, and used local iron and soapstone to make weapons and cooking pots. Soon they were exporting these natural resources, along with woolen and linen cloth.

REINDEER KILLS REINDEER
These arrowheads from Greenland are carved from reindeer antler. Iron was very scarce, so weapons had to be made from the materials at hand. Reindeer were a major source of food, and the settlers may have used these arrows to hunt them.

FIRE AND ICE LAND
Iceland's interior is harsh and inhospitable, with jagged mountains, glaciers, and several active volcanoes. But the coast is green and fertile. In the Viking Age there were also extensive forests between the mountains and the sea. By A.D. 930 the coast was densely populated. The interior was never really inhabited.

West Fjords

Faxa Fjord

Reykjavik

Thingvellir
(Thing Plain)

Mt. Hekla
(volcano)

Vatna Jökull
(huge glacier)

HELGE'S ANIMALS
This elegant piece of carved wood was discovered in the ruins of a house in Greenland. It dates from the 11th century. It may be the arm of a chair, or a tiller used to steer a boat (pp. 9, 11). The surface is carved with with big-eyed animals that look like cats. A runic inscription at the end probably proclaims the owner's name, Helge.

America

Leif the Lucky, Erik the Red's son, also discovered land by accident when his ships went off course on a trip to Greenland. Around the year 1001, he became the first European to set foot on North America, probably in Newfoundland, Canada. He called it Vinland, "Wine Land." This strange name may come from giant huckleberries that Leif thought were red grapes. The Vikings also discovered Markland ("Wood Land") and Helluland ("Rock Land"). These may be Labrador and Baffin Island to the north.

VIKINGS IN VINLAND
Evidence of Viking settlements in North America includes one located at L'Anse aux Meadows in Newfoundland, and to the north on Ellesmere Island. Large houses with thick sod walls have been unearthed. Viking objects, including a dress pin, a spindle whorl (p. 44), and a coin have been found. It is possible the Vikings sailed farther south along Nova Scotia to the New England coast of what is now the state of Maine.

odern tapestry showing Leif the Lucky sighting Vinland

EXPLORING THE FROZEN NORTH
is rune stone was found at Kingiktorsuak, Greenland, at latitude 73° North. This means that settlers must have explored the frozen north of the island. The stone was arved around the year 1300. The Viking community in Greenland died out not too long after this date.

GREENLAND INUIT
The Inuit (Eskimos) made everything they needed from the natural resources of the land and sea. But the Vikings had to import timber, iron, and corn to survive.

Greenland

ost of this inhospitable island covered in ice and snow. Erik e Red called it "Greenland" to courage people to move there. ne Vikings made two settlements, the eastern and western ttlements, in the two areas here the land could be farmed. ey built their farms on the edges fjords, often far inland. They farmed eep and cattle, but depended mainly reindeer and seals for food.

Animal head

WHALEBONE AXE
The Inuit in Greenland made weapons from the bones of seals, whales, and reindeer. This whalebone axehead from a Viking farm shows that the Vikings did the same. Its shape is very similar to iron axeheads (p. 15), but it wouldn't have been as strong. It was probably a toy made for a child.

Animal with gaping jaws and huge teeth

A Viking fort

THE VIKINGS BUILT FOUR great circular forts in Denmark. Two of them, at Aggersborg and Fyrkat, are on the Jutland peninsula. The other two are at Trelleborg on the island of Sjælland and Nonnebakken on the island of Fyn. It was thought that King Svein Forkbeard built them to help launch his invasion of England in 1013. But dendrochronology – a dating method based on the growth rings in trees – shows that the forts were built earlier, around 980. It is now thought that King Harald Bluetooth had them constructed to unify his kingdom and strengthen his rule. Bones dug up in cemeteries outside the ramparts prove that women and children lived there as well as men. Some of the fort buildings were workshops, where smiths forged weapons and jewelry from gold, silver, and iron.

THE WALLS GO UP
The first step in building a fort was clearing th land and preparing the timber. This detail fro a 15th-century Byzantine manuscript shows Swedish Vikings making the walls of Novgor in Russia in the 10th century.

Aerial photograph of the site of the Trelleborg fortress

TRELLEBORG, FROM THE AIR
The forts had a strict geometrical layout. Each one lay withir high circular rampart, a mound of earth and turf held up by wooden framework. This was divided into four quadrants t two roads, one running north–south, the other east–west. Fo long houses sat in a square in each of the quadrants. The roa were paved with timber. Covered gateways, which may ha been topped with towers, were placed where the roads met rampart. The largest fort, Aggersborg, was 790 ft (240 m) i diameter. Trelleborg was much smaller, 445 ft (136 m) acros Trelleborg is unusual because 15 extra houses were built outs the main fort. These were protected by their own rampart. A four forts were built on important land routes, possibly so th Harald could keep an eye on the area in case of rebellion.

Two roads criss-crossing fort

River

Cemetery

Houses

Circular ramparts built of earth and turf and faced with wood

Extra outer rampart

Ditch

Four houses around a square yard

Layout of the Trelleborg fortress

TRELLEBORG HOUSE, SIDE VIEW
The buildings at the forts were made of wood, which rotted away a long time ago. All that is left are ghostly outlines and black holes where the posts once stood. This replica of a house was built in 1948. It is 96 ft 5 in (29.4 m) long. The elegant curving roof is "hogbacked" in shape. House-shaped gravestones and caskets from England give an idea of how it once looked. Experts now believe that there was only one roof that reached all the way down to the short outer posts.

Iron blade, badly rusted now

Silver inlaid in geometric patterns

Gables decorated with projections called finials

THE COMPLETE WORKS OF HARALD BLUETOOTH
The four forts were only one of King Harald Bluetooth's huge projects that left his mark on the Danish landscape. His engineering works include the first bridge in Scandinavia, a huge wooden structure at Ravning Enge in Jútland. He also strengthened the Danevirke, a massive wall that protected Denmark from invasion from the south. And he built a grand memorial at Jelling in Jutland (above). This includes the Jelling Stone, the biggest and grandest of Viking memorial stones (pp. 60–61).

GUARDING THE FORT
Various weapons have been found at the forts. This beautiful T-shaped axehead (p. 15) comes from a grave at Trelleborg. It was probably a symbol of power, not a working weapon. A light throwing spear was found in a guardhouse at the Fyrkat fortress.

TRELLEBORG HOUSE, FRONT VIEW
The houses were built of upright staves (wooden planks) set straight into the earth. They all followed a standard pattern. The main door at each end opened into a small room. These led in turn into a huge central living room where a big fire always burned. Farmhouses like the ones excavated at Vorbasse in Jutland have a similar layout. The wood must have rotted quickly, and there is no evidence of repairs. The forts were probably only inhabited for a few years. King Harald was forced into exile in 986. Soon after this date, the forts he had built were left to rot.

Sturdy wooden posts hold up roof

lls made of staves (planks)

Main door

Smoke hole over fire that burned in a hearth in the middle of the central living room

Roof is covered in overlapping shingles (wooden tiles)

Finials

Other ships

BRONZE AGE BOATS
Rock carvings in Sweden and Norway show boats from as early as 1800 B.C. Sails were developed in Scandinavia just before the Viking Age, around A.D. 700. Before then, all ships were rowed.

THE VIKINGS BUILT SHIPS and boats of many shapes and sizes, suited to different waters and uses. They were all variations on the same design, with overlapping strakes (planks), a keel, and matching prow and stern. Only the longest, fastest vessels were taken raiding. Cargo ships were slower and wider, with lots of room for storing goods. Other boats were specially made for sailing in narrow inlets and rivers, for following the coast, or for crossing oceans. There were fishing boats, ferries for carrying passengers across rivers and fjords, and small boats designed for lakes. Small rowing boats were also carried on board larger boats.

LEIF SIGHTS AMERICA
Explorers sailed wide-bodied, sturdy ships. These w[ere] much heavier than warships and had more space f[or] passengers and their belongings and supplies. In th[e] dramatic interpretation of Leif the Lucky's voyage [to] America (p. 21), Leif is shown pointing in wonder a[t the] new continent. His other hand holds the tiller. The[y] raised deck at the stern (back) can be clearly seen. Leif was Erik the Red's son (p. 20), and is also known[as] Leif Eriksson.

Steering oar

Two sets of oars

ROWING BOAT
Rowing boats were made just like miniature ships. This is a replica of one of the three small rowing boats buried with the Gokstad ship (pp. 8–9). It had two pairs of slender oars and a stubby steering oar.

Hole for rope

CARGO S[HIP]
This is the prow of [one] of the five ships fr[om] Roskilde Fjord, Denm[ark] (pp. 10–11). It is a merch[ant] ship, 45 ft 3 in (13.8 m) l[ong] and 10 ft 10 in (3.3 m) w[ide] and probably made locally[. It] could carry five tons of car[go]. This would have been stow[ed] in the center of the ship a[nd] covered with animal hides [to] protect it from the rain. The cr[ew] could still steer and work the [sail] from decks at the prow and ste[rn]. The ship may have belonged [to a] merchant who sailed along the coas[t of] Norway to pick up iron and soapst[one] or across the Baltic Sea in searc[h of] luxuries like amb[er]

Forward oar-port (hole for oar)

Gunwale, top strake

A copy of the prow (below) in place

Overlapping strakes held together with iron nails or bolts

ONE-PIECE
The cargo ship above is put together with great skill. The shipbuilder carved the entire prow from a single piece of oak. The keel was made first. Then the prow and stern were nailed to the keel. Finally the strakes and deck boards were fitted.

The lines of the strakes are continued on the prow in elegant carvings

DROPPING ANCHOR
Every ship needs an anchor. The anchor of the Oseberg ship (pp. 54–57) was solid iron with an oak frame. It weighed 22 lb (10 kg). This stone anchor comes from Iceland.

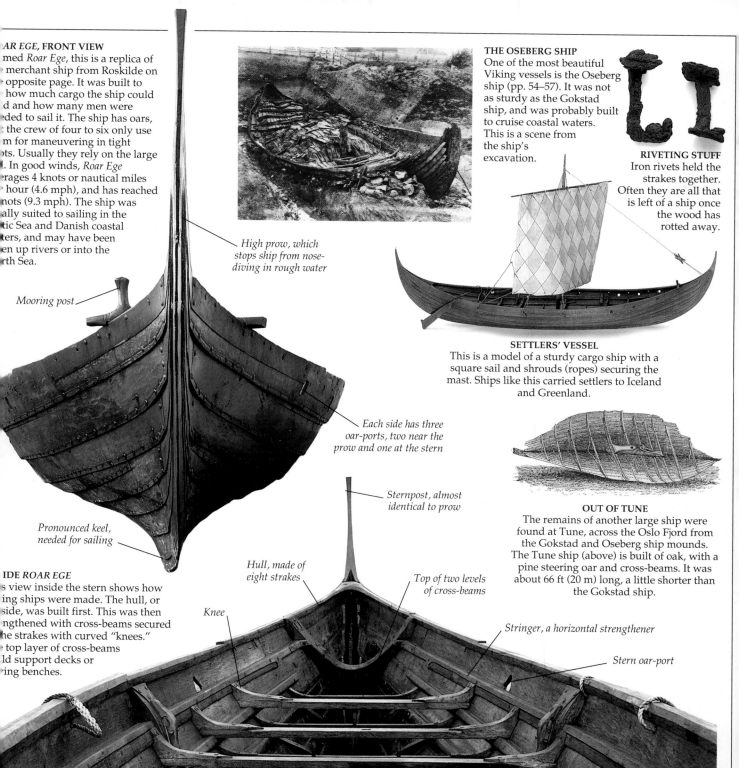

AR EGE, FRONT VIEW

...med *Roar Ege*, this is a replica of ...merchant ship from Roskilde on ...opposite page. It was built to ...how much cargo the ship could ...d and how many men were ...ded to sail it. The ship has oars, ...t the crew of four to six only use ...m for maneuvering in tight ...ts. Usually they rely on the large ...l. In good winds, *Roar Ege* ...rages 4 knots or nautical miles ...hour (4.6 mph), and has reached ...nots (9.3 mph). The ship was ...ally suited to sailing in the ...tic Sea and Danish coastal ...ters, and may have been ...en up rivers or into the ...rth Sea.

Mooring post

High prow, which stops ship from nose-diving in rough water

Each side has three oar-ports, two near the prow and one at the stern

Pronounced keel, needed for sailing

THE OSEBERG SHIP
One of the most beautiful Viking vessels is the Oseberg ship (pp. 54–57). It was not as sturdy as the Gokstad ship, and was probably built to cruise coastal waters. This is a scene from the ship's excavation.

RIVETING STUFF
Iron rivets held the strakes together. Often they are all that is left of a ship once the wood has rotted away.

SETTLERS' VESSEL
This is a model of a sturdy cargo ship with a square sail and shrouds (ropes) securing the mast. Ships like this carried settlers to Iceland and Greenland.

OUT OF TUNE
The remains of another large ship were found at Tune, across the Oslo Fjord from the Gokstad and Oseberg ship mounds. The Tune ship (above) is built of oak, with a pine steering oar and cross-beams. It was about 66 ft (20 m) long, a little shorter than the Gokstad ship.

IDE *ROAR EGE*

...s view inside the stern shows how ...ing ships were made. The hull, or ...side, was built first. This was then ...ngthened with cross-beams secured ...he strakes with curved "knees." ...e top layer of cross-beams ...ld support decks or ...ing benches.

Sternpost, almost identical to prow

Hull, made of eight strakes

Top of two levels of cross-beams

Knee

Stringer, a horizontal strengthener

Stern oar-port

Trading east and west

THE VIKINGS WERE GREAT TRADERS who traveled far beyond Scandinavia buying and selling goods. The riches of the North included timber for ship-building; iron for making tools and weapons; furs for warm clothing; skins from whales and seals for ship ropes; and whale bones and walrus ivory for carving. These were carried to far-flung places and exchanged for local goods. Traders would return from Britain with wheat, silver, and cloth, and bring wine, salt, pottery, and gold back from the Mediterranean. They sailed across the Baltic Sea and upriver into Russia, then continued on foot or camel as far as Constantinople (now Istanbul) and Jerusalem. In markets all along the way, they haggled over the price of glass, exotic spices, silks, and slaves. Some Viking market towns grew to be important trade centers, such as Birka in Sweden, Kaupang in Norway, Hedeby in Denmark, York in England, Dublin in Ireland, and Kiev in Ukraine.

THE SLAVE TRADE
Some Vikings made their fortune trading slaves. They took many Christian prisoners, like this 9th-century French monk. Some slaves were taken home for heavy farm and building work. Others were sold for silver to Arab countries.

Coin and die for striking (making) coins, from York, England

Three early Danish coins

THE COMING OF COINS
Coins only became common toward the end of the Viking Age. Before then, goods were usually bought with pieces of silver or bartered – swapped for items of similar value. The first Danish coins were made in the 9th century. But it wasn't until 975, under King Harald Bluetooth, that coins were made in large numbers.

Brass Buddha-like figure

Colorful enamel

Bands of brass

MADE IN ENGLAND?
One of the many beautiful objects found with the Oseberg ship (pp. 54–57) was the mysterious "Buddha bucket." Its handle is attached to two brass figures with crossed legs that look just like Buddhas. But the Vikings were not Buddhists, and the craftsmanship suggests that the figures were made in England. So how did the splendid bucket end up in a queen's grave in Norway? It must have been traded and brought back from England.

Staves (strips) of yew wood

RHINE GLASS
Only rich Vikings drank from glass cups. Many have been found in Swedish graves. This glass must have been bought or stolen in the Rhineland, in modern Germany.

TUSK, TUSK

The Vikings hunted walruses for their hide, which was turned into ship ropes. The large animals were skinned in a spiral, starting from the tail. Traders also sold the animal's ivory tusks, either unworked or beautifully carved.

Spruce-wood stick

Twelve unfinished
iron axeheads

Fur hat

CUTTING THE AXE

These unfinished axeheads on a spruce stick were found on a Danish beach. They may have washed ashore from a wrecked trading ship bringing cargo to Denmark. Spruce does not grow in Denmark, so they probably came from Sweden or Norway, where there is plenty of spruce and iron. Danish craftsmen were going to finish work on the axes.

Warm wool cape

Brooch to hold
cloak in place

Thor's hammer

Cross

Copper wire

Amber beads
used in
jewelry

Knife in
leather sheath

Bronze bowls

IN THE BALANCE

Trader's scales have been found all over the Viking world. This handy set of folding scales could be stored in a small bronze case when not in use. It was found on the island of Gotland in Sweden.

Bronze case for
set of scales

Long wool tunic
with embroidered
borders

VIKING TRADER

This trader is selling amber, the fossilized resin of trees. Amber was one of Scandinavia's biggest exports. It was traded as beads or in its natural state. Many traders converted to Christianity to make dealings with Christian countries easier. But they often kept faith with pagan gods as well, to make extra sure of protection. This trader wears both a Christian cross and a hammer, the symbol of the god Thor (pp. 7, 54–55).

Trousers of
woolen cloth

WEIGHING SILVER

Before coins, goods were bought with hack silver – chopped up pieces of jewelry and coins. This trader is weighing hack silver in a scale.

Symbol showing weight

TRADER'S WEIGHTS

These five weights from Hemlingby in Sweden seem to form a complete set. Each one is stamped with a different number of tiny circles. These probably represent their weight, from half an öre to 1, 3, 4, and 5 örtugar. The örtugar was equivalent to 3 öre or around 0.3 oz (8 g).

Iron weight with
brass coating

Leather shoes, laced
up around the ankle

Kings and freemen

VIKING SOCIETY HAD THREE CLASSES – slaves, freemen, and nobles. Most of the hard labor was done by slaves, or *thralls*. Many were foreigners captured in war (p. 26). Wealthy people sometimes had their slaves killed and buried with them. Slaves could be freed. Freemen included farmers, traders, craftsmen, warriors, and big landowners. At the beginning of the Viking Age, there were many local chieftains (nobles) who ruled over small areas. They were subject to the rule of the Thing, the local assembly where all freemen could voice their opinions and complain about others. But chieftains and kings gradually increased their wealth and power by raiding and conquering foreign lands. By the end of the Viking Age, around A.D. 1050, Norway, Denmark, and Sweden were each ruled by a single, powerful king, and the role of the Things had declined.

WELL-GROOMED
The well-off Viking warrior or chieftain took pride in his appearance. This Viking carved from elk antler has neatly trimmed hair and beard.

PEASANT WARR
This peasant was not rich, dressed simply. But he w freeman, and owned his own fa which his wife would look a when he went to war. The 1 century poem *Rigspula* descri a peasant who makes furni and his wife who wea They have a called Karl, wl means farmer or f man. Karl's v wears fine goats and carries key symbol of status (p.

Simple leather belt

Wooden axe-handle

Plain iron axehead

Wooden sh with iron

Plain wool trous

Leather shoes

Toggle (fastener) made of leather

Goatskin leather

BEST FOOT FORWARD
Leather shoes for rich or poor were of simple design. Fancy pairs were colored or had ornamental seams or even inscriptions. The most common leather for shoes was goatskin.

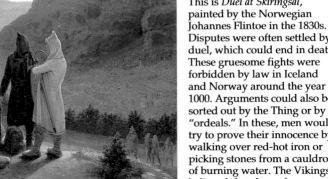

FIGHTING IT OUT
This is *Duel at Skiringsal*, painted by the Norwegian Johannes Flintoe in the 1830s. Disputes were often settled by a duel, which could end in death. These gruesome fights were forbidden by law in Iceland and Norway around the year 1000. Arguments could also be sorted out by the Thing or by "ordeals." In these, men would try to prove their innocence by walking over red-hot iron or picking stones from a cauldron of burning water. The Vikings believed that the gods protected the innocent.

FANCY HAT
The rich wore expensive clothes and imported jewelry. These parts of an elaborate cap were made in Kiev in Ukraine and worn by a nobleman in Birka, Sweden.

Silver cap mount

Silver tassels

Braids for fastening cloak

Wool tunic embroidered with animals and faces

MAMMEN CHIEFTAIN
Fine clothes, tablecloths, white bread, and silver cups were all signs of nobility. This man is wearing a reconstruction of clothes found in a nobleman's grave in Mammen, Denmark. They are made of high-quality wool and silk, decorated with embroidered borders and even gold and silver thread. The noble couple in the poem *Rigspula* have a son called Iarl, which means earl. He owns land, rides horses, and can read and write runes (pp. 58–59). His wife Erna is slender and wise. Their youngest child is called Konr ungr, which means king.

Cloak of dyed wool with embroidered borders

TO CAP IT OFF
This silk cap was worn by a rich man or woman in the Viking town of York, England. The silk may have been imported from faraway Constantinople.

Cloak embroidered with human faces

BORDER FACES
The border of the Mammen cloak was a panel of imported silk embroidered with human faces. No one knows whose faces these are. But the beautiful decoration shows how wealthy the wearer was.

Bronze brooch for holding cloak in place

Tunic was often worn over linen undershirt

Dyed woolen trousers

Fur trim

THINGS AND ALTHINGS
Each district had its own assembly, or Thing. Meetings were held outside at a special spot. This is a 19th-century painting of the Icelandic Althing, held once a year (p. 20). One observer said that "Icelanders have no king, only the law."

Bronze belt buckle

BROOCHES AND BUCKLES
All Viking men wore brooches and buckles to fasten their clothes. But the richer they were, the more ornate their brooch or buckle. These come from Gotland, Sweden.

Women and children

VIKING WOMEN WERE INDEPENDENT. While the men were away on expeditions, women ran households and farms. A woman could choose her own husband, and could sue for divorce if he beat her or was unfaithful. On runestones (pp. 58–59), women were praised for their good housekeeping or skill in handiwork such as embroidery. Wealthy women raised runestones and paid for bridges to be built. Viking children had no school. Instead they worked in the fields and workshops, and helped with cooking, spinning, and weaving. Not all women and children stayed home. Many joined their husbands or fathers in colonies such as England. They hid somewhere safe during battles, and came out later to help set up new villages.

BRYNHILD
This is a romantic engraving of Brynhild. According to legend, she was a Valkyrie, a mythical woman warrior (p. 53). In reality, there is no evidence that any Viking women were warriors, or even traders or craftsworkers. But one female scald (poet) and a female rune carver are known.

TOY HORSE
About 900 years ago, a small boy or girl in Trondheim, Norway, played with this toy horse made of wood. Children also had toy boats. They played board games and made music with small pipes (p. 50). In the summer young Vikings swam and played ball; in the winter they skated and played in the snow.

Two carved animal heads with open jaws

STARTING YOUNG
Viking boys played with toy weapons made of wood. They probably began serious weapon practice in their early teens. Some young men seem to have gone raiding when they were as young as sixteen.

Piece of leat covers point, boys will hurt each ot

Toy sp made of wo

Woolen tunic with embroidered collar

Leathe ba

Decorated belt tip

Toy sword

BONE SMOOTH
One of a woman's main responsibilities was making clothes for the whole family (pp. 44–45). After she had woven a piece of linen, a woman probably stretched it across a smoothing board and rubbed it with a glass ball until it was smooth and shiny. This board from Norway is made of whalebone.

30

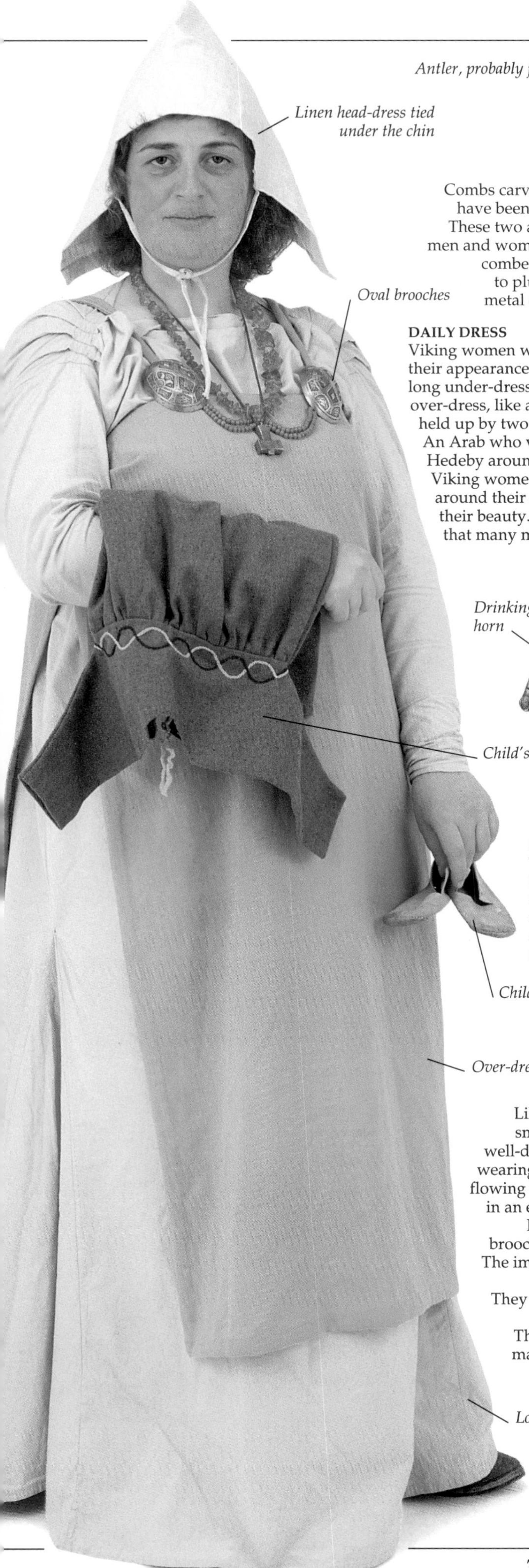

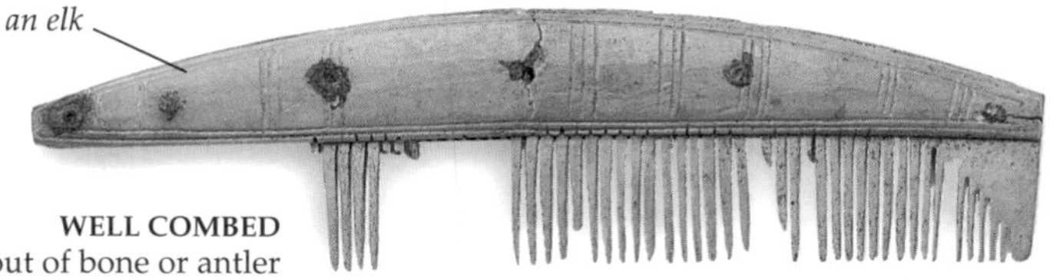

Linen head-dress tied
under the chin

Antler, probably from an elk

WELL COMBED
Combs carved out of bone or antler
have been found all over the Viking world.
These two are from Birka in Sweden. Viking
men and women made sure their hair was well
combed. They also used metal tweezers
to pluck out unwanted hairs, and tiny
metal ear scoops to clean out their ears.

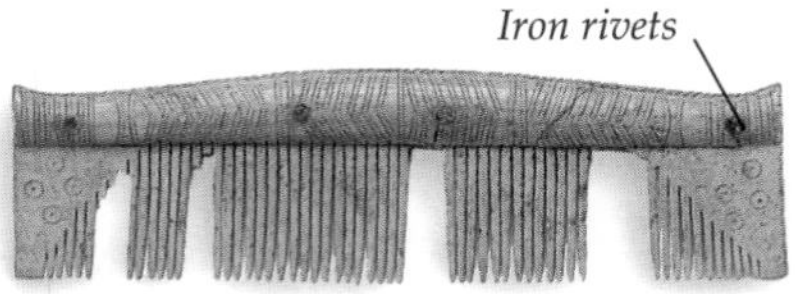

Iron rivets

Oval brooches

DAILY DRESS
Viking women were very particular about
their appearance. This woman is wearing a
long under-dress. On top she has a short
over-dress, like a pinafore dress. This is
held up by two oval brooches.
An Arab who visited the town of
Hedeby around A.D. 950 said that
Viking women wore make-up
around their eyes to increase
their beauty. He also noted
that many men did the same.

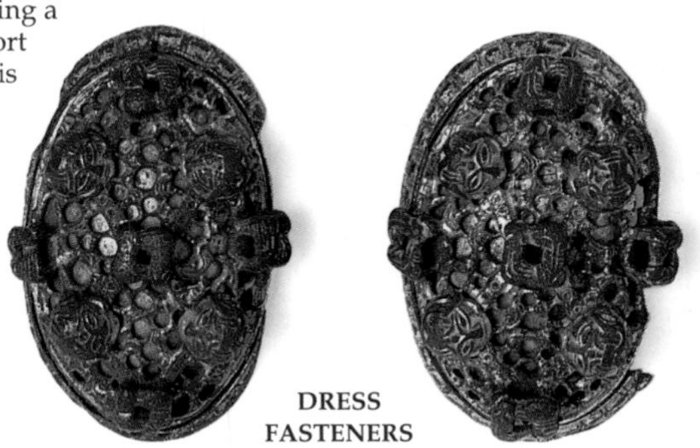

Hair tied in bun

Drinking
horn

DRESS
FASTENERS
Oval brooches were only worn
by women. This pair comes from Ågerup in
Denmark. Finding such brooches in a grave shows
that the dead person was a woman. Although the
cloth of the dress has usually rotted away, the
position of the brooches on the shoulders shows
how they were worn.

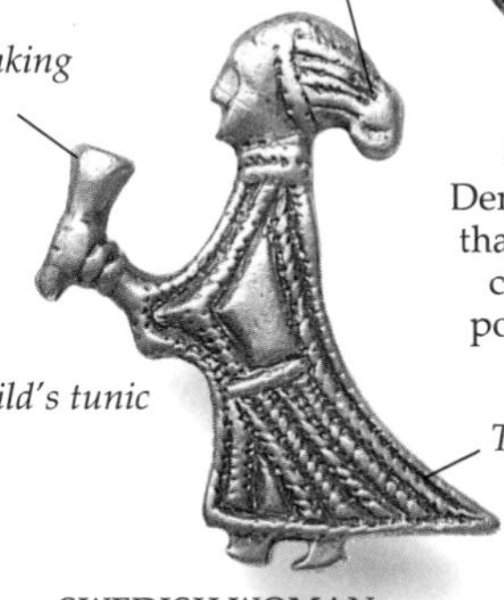

Child's tunic

Train of dress

SWEDISH WOMAN
This silver pendant is from
Birka, Sweden. It is in the
shape of a woman in a dress
with a triangular train. She is
carrying a drinking horn, and
may be a Valkyrie (p. 53).

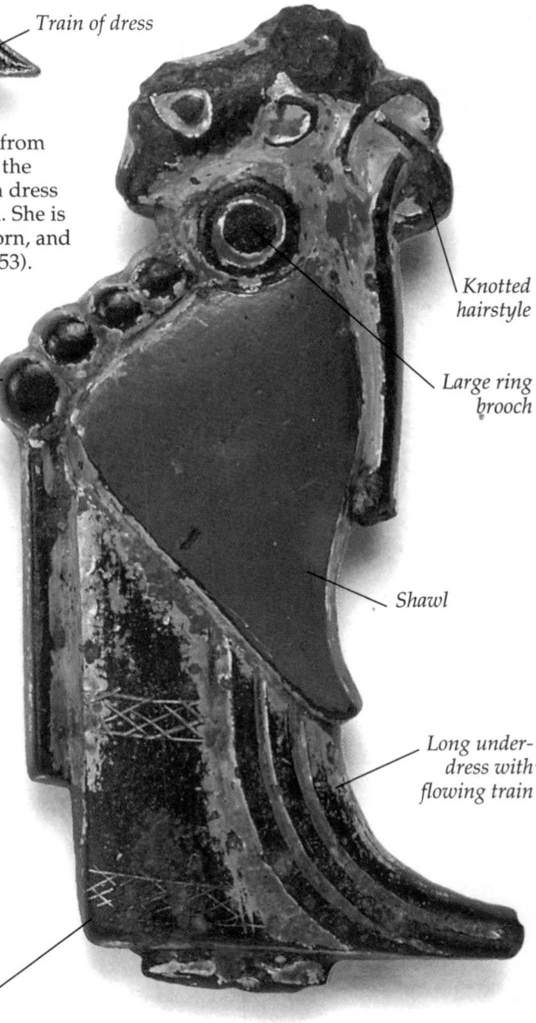

Child's shoes

Knotted
hairstyle

Large ring
brooch

Bead necklace

ALL DRESSED UP
Like the one above, this
small pendant shows a
well-dressed woman. She is
wearing a shawl over a long,
flowing dress. Her hair is tied
in an elegant, knotted style.
Her beads and a large
brooch are easy to identify.
The importance of pendants
like these is unclear.
They could have had some
magical meaning.
The figures represented
may even be goddesses.

Over-dress

Shawl

Long under-
dress with
flowing train

Long under-dress

Over-dress decorated
with woven bands

At home

HOME LIFE REVOLVED around a central hall or living room. The layout was much the same all over the Viking world. A long, open hearth (fireplace) burned in the center, with a smoke hole in the ceiling above. The floor was stamped earth. The people sat and slept on raised platforms along the curved walls. Pillows and cushions stuffed with duck down or chicken feathers made this more comfortable. Well-off homes might have a few pieces of wooden furniture and a chest for precious belongings. Houses often had smaller rooms for cooking or spinning on either side of the main hall. Small buildings with low floors dug out of the ground were used as workshops, weaving sheds, animal barns, or houses for the poor. A chieftain's hall could be lined with wall hangings or carved or painted wooden panels. Around the year 1000, an Icelandic poet described panels decorated with scenes of gods and legends in the hall of a great chieftain. The poem was called *Húsdrápa*, which means "poem in praise of the house."

HOUSES, ICELANDIC STYLE
Good timber was scarce in Iceland and other North Atlantic islands (pp. 20–21). So houses usually had stone foundations, and walls and roofs made of turf. Some houses were dug into the ground, which kept them warm in winter and cool in summer. The walls were lined with wooden paneling to keep out the cold and damp.

Planks carved with beautiful animal heads

Slats join sideboards

SWEET DREAMS
Only the rich had chairs or beds. Ordinary Vikings sat on benches or stools or on the floor. At night, they stretched out on rugs on raised platforms. The wealthy woman in the Oseberg ship (pp. 54–57) was buried with not one, but three beds. This is a replica of the finest one. It is made of beech wood. The headboard planks are carved in the form of animal heads with arching necks (p. 9). The woman probably slept on a feather mattress, and was kept warm by a quilt filled with down or feathers.

Small window with no glass that may have had shutters

Turf roof was green with grass in summer, and covered with snow in winter

End view of Trondheim house

TRONDHEIM HOUSE
This is a model of a house built in Trondheim, Norway, in the year 1003. Its walls are horizontal logs notched and fitted together at the corners. A layer of birchbark was laid on the pointed roof and covered in turf. The bark would have kept the water out, while the earth and grass acted as insulation. Houses were built in various other ways, depending on local traditions and the materials at hand. Wooden walls were often made of upright posts, or staves, as in the Danish forts (pp. 22–23). Others had walls of wattle (interwoven branches) smeared with daub (clay or dung) to make them waterproof. Roofs could be covered in shingles (wooden tiles), thatch, turf, or matted reeds.

Side view of Trondheim house

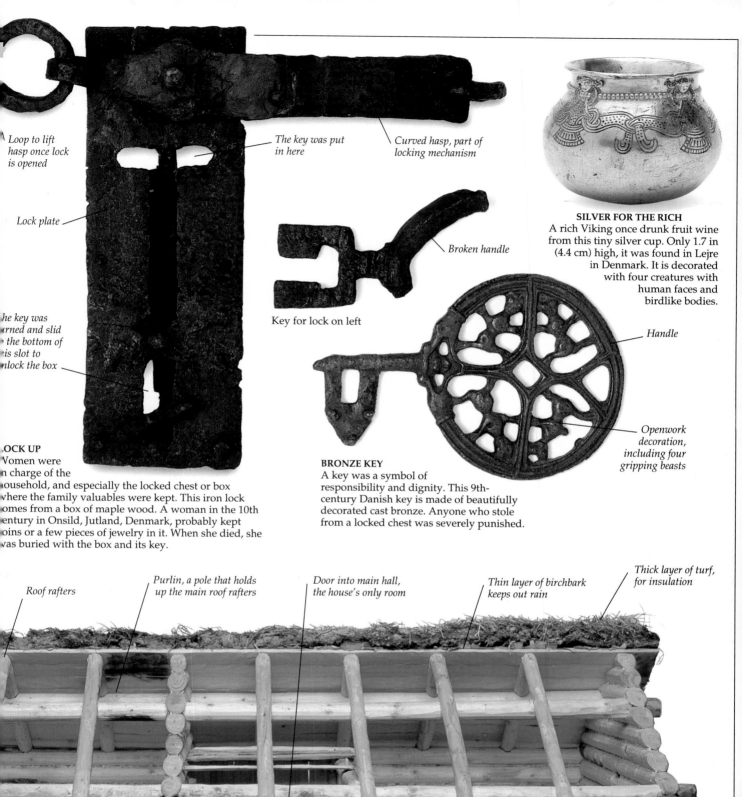

Loop to lift hasp once lock is opened

The key was put in here

Curved hasp, part of locking mechanism

Lock plate

he key was urned and slid the bottom of is slot to nlock the box

SILVER FOR THE RICH
A rich Viking once drunk fruit wine from this tiny silver cup. Only 1.7 in (4.4 cm) high, it was found in Lejre in Denmark. It is decorated with four creatures with human faces and birdlike bodies.

Broken handle

Key for lock on left

Handle

Openwork decoration, including four gripping beasts

OCK UP
Women were n charge of the ousehold, and especially the locked chest or box where the family valuables were kept. This iron lock omes from a box of maple wood. A woman in the 10th entury in Onsild, Jutland, Denmark, probably kept oins or a few pieces of jewelry in it. When she died, she was buried with the box and its key.

BRONZE KEY
A key was a symbol of responsibility and dignity. This 9th-century Danish key is made of beautifully decorated cast bronze. Anyone who stole from a locked chest was severely punished.

Roof rafters

Purlin, a pole that holds up the main roof rafters

Door into main hall, the house's only room

Thin layer of birchbark keeps out rain

Thick layer of turf, for insulation

Mealtime

ALL DAY LONG, the fire in the hearth was kept burning for cooking and heating. The hole in the roof above the fire didn't work very well, so Viking houses were always full of smoke. Rich households had baking ovens in separate rooms. These were heated by placing hot stones inside them. When darkness fell, work on the farm or in the workshop had to stop, and people would gather for the main meal of the day. The rich and the poor ate very different meals, served in different ways. For instance, most Vikings drank beer made from malted barley and hops. But while the poor drank from wooden mugs, the rich used drinking horns with fancy metal rims. They also enjoyed wine imported in barrels from Germany.

NORMAN FEAST
This feast scene from the Bayeux Tapestry (p. 10) shows a table laden with food and dishes. Wealthy Vikings had richly decorated knives and spoons and imported pottery cups and jugs. Ordinary people ate and drank from wooden bowls and cups.

FOOD FROM THE SEA
The sea was full of fish. For Vikings who lived near the coast, fish was the staple food. The bones of cod, herring, and haddock have been found in many Viking settlements. People also caught eels and freshwater fish, such as trout, in the many rivers and lakes that criss-cross Scandinavia.

HOME GROWN
Cabbages (above) and peas were most common vegetables. Most Vikings grew their own.

Pine tree, source of kernels and bark

Dried peas

DRIED COD
Food had to be preserved so it would keep through the winter. Fish and meat were hung in the wind to dry. They could also be pickled in salt water. Salt was collected by boiling sea water, a boring job usually given to slaves. Fish and meat were probably also smoked.

PEAS AND PINE BARK
Poor Vikings made bread with whatever they could find. One loaf found in Sweden contained dried peas and pine bark.

Cumin, a spice found in the Oseberg burial

FIT FOR A QUEEN
Horseradish was one of the seasonings found in the Oseberg burial (pp. 54–57), along with wheat, oats, and fruit.

A Norman cook lifts chunks of cooked meat off the stove with a two-pronged fork

BAKING BREAD
Bread was kneaded in wooden troughs. Then it was baked on a griddle over a fire (as in this 16th-century Swedish picture) or in a pan that sat in the embers. Barley bread was most common, but rich people had loaves made of finer wheat flour.

POACHED EGGS
In the Atlantic islands, Viking settlers gathered gulls' eggs for eating. They also roasted the gulls.

GARLIC BULB
Like modern cooks, the Vikings added garlic and onion to meat stews and soups.

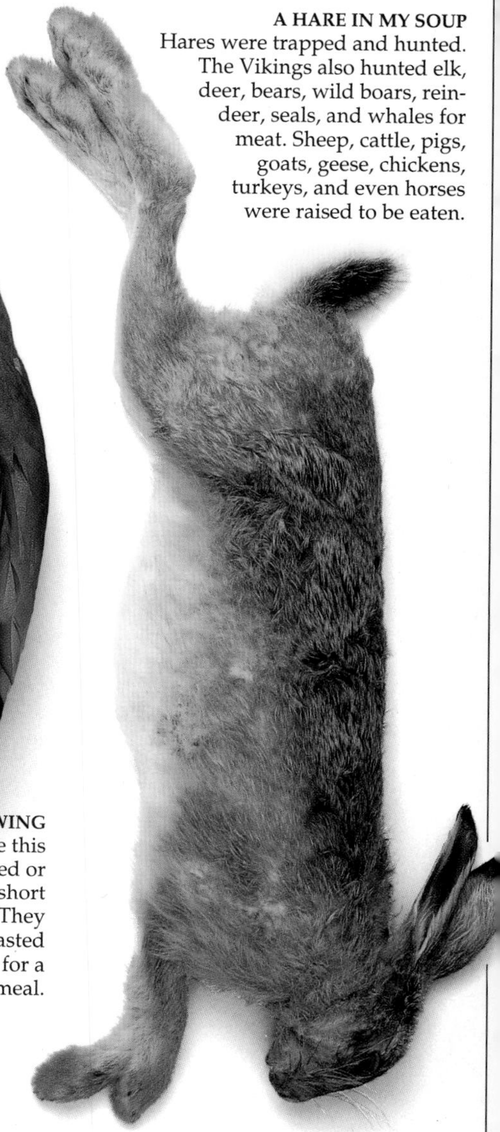

A HARE IN MY SOUP
Hares were trapped and hunted. The Vikings also hunted elk, deer, bears, wild boars, reindeer, seals, and whales for meat. Sheep, cattle, pigs, goats, geese, chickens, turkeys, and even horses were raised to be eaten.

Suspension loop

Iron handle

COOKING CAULDRON
Food was prepared around the hearth in the center of the living room. Meat was stewed in cauldrons, or huge pots, made of iron or soapstone. Some cauldrons were hung over the fire on a chain from the roof-beam. Others, like this one from the Oseberg ship, were suspended from a tripod.

CAUGHT ON THE WING
Game birds like this duck were trapped or hunted with short arrows. They would be roasted on a spit for a tasty meal.

One of the tripod's three legs

Raspberry

Blackberry

BERRY TASTY
Berries and wild fruits such as apples, cherries, and plums were gathered in the summer. Vikings may have grown fruit trees in gardens as well as picking fruit wild in the forest.

*pronged feet
e stuck into the
h floor to keep
cauldron stable*

Iron cauldron

Old crack *Repair holes*

BAYEUX BARBECUE
In this scene from the Bayeux Tapestry (p. 10), two Norman cooks heat a cauldron. The fire sits in a tray like a barbecue. To the left, a third man lifts cooked chunks of meat off a stove onto a plate. The Vikings may have cooked in similar ways.

PATCHED
This clay cooking pot has four holes where a patch was stuck over a crack.

Animals, wild and imagined

BROWN BEAR
Bears were hunted in the far north. Their skins were made into jackets and cloaks, and their claws and teeth were worn as pendants. Warriors may have thought that some of the bear's strength and courage would rub off on them (p. 14).

Bears, wolves, mink, foxes, deer, and wild boar all roamed the dark forests of Norway and Sweden. Whales, otters, seals, walruses, and reindeer lived in the far north. Sea birds flocked along the coasts, and game birds were common inland. Viking legends are also stocked with these animals, most of which were hunted for their meat. They made clothes and bedding from the feathers, furs, and hides, and bones and tusks were raw materials for jewelry, tools, and everyday objects like knife handles. Many of the finest objects were then traded (pp. 26–27). But the animals that they decorated jewelry, tools, and weapons with are not real. Viking craftspeople imagined fantastic and acrobatic creatures. Animal hips become spirals, and plant shoots spring from their bodies. Some beasts become ribbons that twist around each other in intricate patterns.

BRONZE BEAST
This fierce animal with snarling teeth comes from a horse's harness bow (p. 43). It may have been made to scare enemies and protect the horse and wagon.

Head of animal

ST
Elk, deer, and reind all have big antl Craftsmen sawed a carved these to cre combs (p.31). Deer s was used for clot and possibly wall a bed coverir Venison (d meat) was a dried, roast and ea

Bronze, in a mol

FANTASTIC ANIMAL
This brooch from Norway is in the shape of a slender, snake-like animal. It is caught up in a thin ribbon twisting in a fantastic pattern. This is known as the Urnes style of Viking art, after wood carvings on a church at Urnes in Norway.

Gilt (gold-coated) silver

Owl

Bird of prey

BIRD BROOCH
This brooch was found in a woman's grave in Birka, Sweden. It once decorated a belt worn by someone living in Eastern Europe by the river Volga (pp. 18–19). A Viking took it home to Sweden, where a jeweler converted it into a brooch. The birds are quite realistic, and the species are easy to identify. A Viking craftsman would have turned them into fantastic creatures.

GRIPPING BEAST
The acrobatic "gripping beast" became popular in Viking art in the 9th century. This playful animal writhes and turns inside out, gripping its own legs and even its throat.

Gripping beast from a 9th-century Danish brooch

...like deer, sheep ...not shed their horns ...ry year, so the horns ...bigger with age

Each horn of an old Manx Loghtan ram can weigh 12 oz (350 g) and reach 1 ft 6 in (45 cm) in length

SNAKE CHARM
Snakes were common in Viking lands, and are important in poems and stories (p. 50–51). This silver snake pendant was worn by a Swedish woman as a good luck charm or amulet.

CAROLINGIAN CUP
Craftsmen in other areas based their decoration on real animals. This cup was made further south in the [C]arolingian Empire, in modern France [o]r Germany. It is made of gilt (gold-coated) silver decorated with the figure of a bull-like animal and symmetrical leaves of the acanthus [p]lant. The cup must have been traded [o]r plundered, because it was found in a Viking hoard at Halton Moor, [E]ngland, with a silver neck-ring (p. 47) and a gold pendant (p. 46).

[ ]NE WOLF
[Th]e wolf roamed wild in the mountains of Scandinavia. [Th]en, as now, people were terrified of its eerie howl. In [a] Viking myth of the end of the world, called *Ragnarök*, [the] god Odin is gobbled up by a monstrous wolf, Fenrir [(p.]51). *Ragnarök* means the "Doom of the Gods."

HORNED HELMET
The Manx Loghtan sheep was a common farm animal in the Viking Age. Now it is only found on the Isle of Man, an island between England and Ireland that was colonized by Vikings in the 9th century. Sheep were kept all over the Viking world (pp. 40–41). In mountainous areas, Viking shepherds took their flocks to high pastures for the warm summer months. The Manx Loghtan sheep shed its wool naturally, so it didn't have to be sheared. It grew two, four, or sometimes even six horns.

Farming

MOST VIKINGS WERE FARMERS. They often had to work infertile land in harsh weather. The difficult conditions led many farmers to set sail for faraway lands like Iceland (pp. 20–21), where they hoped to find fertile soil and more space for their animals and crops. Sheep, cows, pigs, goats, horses, poultry, and geese were all raised for eating. The milk of cattle, goats, and sheep was drunk or turned into butter and cheese. Farms often had separate byres, sheds where cattle could pass the winter. Even so, many died of cold or starvation. Rich farms had byres to house a hundred cattle. A man's wealth was often measured in animals. Othere, a merchant from northern Norway, told King Alfred of England that he had 20 cattle, 20 sheep, 20 pigs, and a herd of 600 reindeer. But his main source of income was the furs he traded.

SHEARS
Vikings sheared sheep, cut cloth, and even trimmed beards with iron shears like these.

JARLSHOF FARM
The ruins of a 9th-century Viking farmhouse on the Shetland Islands. It had two rooms, a long hall and a kitchen. The farmers sat and slept on platforms that ran along the curved walls. A hearth burned in the center of the hall.

Thick fleece shed once a year, in spring

Two sickle blades

MILKING REINDEER
This 16th-century Swedish engraving shows a woman milking reindeer. In the far north, people farmed reindeer for their milk, meat, and hides. They were also hunted in many places, including Greenland (pp. 20–21).

BLACK SHEEP
Hebridean sheep were farmed by Vikings on the Hebrides islands. Like Manx Loghtan sheep (p. 37), they shed their wool naturally, and do not have to be sheared. They can live on sparse vegetation and are very hardy.

Ard blade

HARVEST TOOLS
The ground was broken up in the spring with an ard, a simple plow. Grain was cut with iron sickles with wooden handles. The blades of these tools were sharpened with whetstones (sharpening stones).

PLOWING AND SOWING
This detail from the Bayeux Tapestry (p. 10) shows Norm[a]ns plowing (far left) and sowing seeds (left). The Vikings woul[d] have used similar techniques.

FLOUR POWER
Grain was ground into flour with a quern stone. This one comes from a Viking farm at Ribblehead in Yorkshire, England. The grain was placed on the bottom stone. Then the top stone was laid on it and the wooden handle was turned around. Rich Vikings preferred finer flour, ground with querns made of lava imported from the Rhineland in Germany.

op stone

Bottom stone

Ears and grains of spelt wheat

Ground wheat

GRAINS
Spelt is an early form of wheat. The Vikings also grew barley and rye.

LONGHORN COW
Cattle like this were once farmed in many parts of the Viking world. Now that new breeds have been developed, longhorn cattle only survive on a few special farms. Domestic animals weren't just raised for their meat and milk. Sheep's wool, cattle hide, and poultry feathers were also used to make clothes and bedding. Cattle horns are hollow, and are ideal as drinking horns. These were tricky to put down, and had to be rested in special holders. Animal bones were carved into knife handles, combs, pins, needles, even jewelry.

Getting around

WELL GROOMED
A complete wooden wagon was found in the Oseberg burial ship (pp. 54–57). It is the only one known from Viking times. The surface is covered in carvings, including four heads of Viking men. The men all have well-groomed beards and mustaches.

MUCH OF SCANDINAVIA is rugged and mountainous. The large forests, lakes, and marshes make traveling difficult, especially in bad weather. Vikings went by ship whenever possible. Traveling overland was often easiest in winter, when snow covered uneven ground and the many rivers and lakes froze over. People got around on sleighs, skis, and skates. In deep snow, they wore snow-shoes. Large sleighs were pulled by horses. To stop the horses from slipping on the ice, smiths nailed iron crampons, or studs, to their hooves. In the summer, Vikings rode, walked, or traveled in wagons pulled by horses or oxen. Roads were built on high land, to avoid difficult river crossings. The first bridge in Scandinavia, a huge wooden trestle, was built near Jelling in Denmark around the year 979, probably on orders from King Harald Bluetooth.

A GOOD DEED
Christian Vikings thought building roads and bridges would help their souls go heaven. This causeway in Täby, Sweden, was built by Jarlebanke (p. 59). He celebrated his good deed by raising four rune stones.

Bone ice skate from York, England

16th-century engraving of a Swedish couple skiing with single skis, as the Vikings did

ICE-LEGS
The word *ski* is Norwegian. Prehistoric rock carvings in Norway show that people have been skiing there for at least 5,000 years. The Vikings definitely used skis, though none have survived. Ice skates have been found all over the north. The Vikings called them "ice-legs." They were made by tying the leg bones of horses to the bottoms of leather boots. The skater pushed him or herself along with a pointed iron stick like a ski pole.

HORSING AROUN[D]
Vikings were excell[ent] riders. This sil[ver] horseman comes fr[om] Birka in Sweden, a[nd] dates from the 1[0th] century. The ri[der] is wearin[g a] sword, a[nd a] must[ache—] a warri[or]

Beech body decorated in iron studs with tinned heads

One of four carved animal heads

SLED[GE]
This is on[e of] the three f[ine] sledges from [the] Oseberg bu[rial] (pp. 54–57). [The] curved runners [are] carved with beaut[iful] decorations. Lashed on to[p is] an open box. Ferocious ani[mal] heads snarl from the four corn[ers]

Curved oak runners

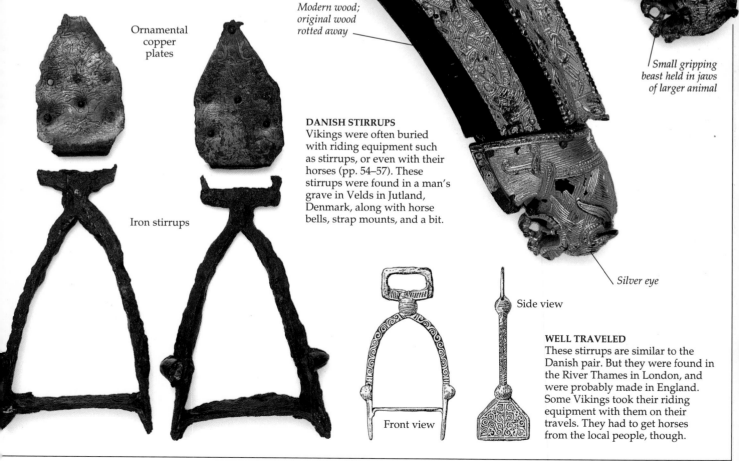

Copper alloy covered in gold

Hole through which
reins passed

Ribbon decoration
in Jellinge style

Animal heads, possibly meant
to scare off evil spirits and stop
horses from bolting

REINING THEM IN
Harness bows were only used in Denmark.
The curved surface rested on a horse's back.
The reins passed through the holes in the center to
stop them from getting tangled up. This pair was
found in a smith's hoard in Mammen, Jutland. They
belonged to a wealthy chieftain, and were probably
only used on ceremonial occasions. Their splendid
decoration shows how wealthy he must have been.

Ornamental
copper
plates

Modern wood;
original wood
rotted away

Small gripping
beast held in jaws
of larger animal

Iron stirrups

DANISH STIRRUPS
Vikings were often buried
with riding equipment such
as stirrups, or even with their
horses (pp. 54–57). These
stirrups were found in a man's
grave in Velds in Jutland,
Denmark, along with horse
bells, strap mounts, and a bit.

Silver eye

Side view

Front view

WELL TRAVELED
These stirrups are similar to the
Danish pair. But they were found in
the River Thames in London, and
were probably made in England.
Some Vikings took their riding
equipment with them on their
travels. They had to get horses
from the local people, though.

In the workshop

T HE VIKINGS PARTLY OWE THEIR SUCCESS to expert craftsmen who made their strong weapons and fast ships. The weapon-smith who forged sharp swords, spears, and axes (pp. 14–15) was the most respected. But the smiths who made the iron tools for working metal and wood were skilled, too. They knew how to work different metals and create elaborate decorations. Smiths also produced everyday objects like locks and keys, cauldrons for cooking, and iron rivets for ships. Highly trained Viking carpenters made a wide range of objects, including ships. They knew exactly what wood to use for what purpose, and how to cut timber to give maximum strength and flexibility. They could carve intricate designs and sometimes painted them with bright colors. Most of the colors have faded now, but enough paint survives to give an idea of the original effect.

Molding iron for making grooves or patterns on planks

PRESSED GOLD
This gold brooch from Hornelund in Denmark was made from a lead die. The jeweler pressed the die into a she of gold to create a pattern. Then he decorated the surface wit gold wire and blobs or granules gold. Only the richest chieftain or kings could afford such a beautiful brooch.

Twisted gold wire forms heart-shaped patterns

One of three heart-shaped loops made of strands of twisted gold wire

Granules of gold

Lead die from Viborg, Denm used for making precious m brooches like the Hornelund b

Plant decoration shows influences from western Europe, but the technique is purely Scandinavian

Plate shears for cutting sheet metal

Smith's tongs for holding hot iron on anvil

MAKING DRAGONS
Bronze was heated in a crucible over a fire until it melted. Then the smith poured it into the stone mold. When the metal cooled, he lifted out a fine dragon head with a curly mane. It may have decorated a fancy box. A stone mold like this one could be used over and over again. Many brooches and dress pins (pp. 48–49) were cast in similar molds.

Modern casting

Stone m for bro dragon he from Birka, Swed

ht hammerhead

avy hammer-
d

AXES AND ADZES
The carpenter used an axe to fell (cut down) trees and chop off their branches. He then used a T-shaped axe (p. 15) to shape and smooth the planks. An adze has its blade at right angles to the handle. The carpenter could shape a log by chipping away at its surface with an adze.

Hole for wooden haft (handle)

Felling a tree with an axe

ze head

THING A SWORD
carving is part of a
-century doorway
the church in
stad, Norway (p. 51).
ows the hero Sigurd
king a sword the smith Regin
made for him. In another
ing, Regin holds the hot iron
a pair of tongs and hits it
a hammer. A helper works
ellows to keep the fire in the
e burning.

Wood is modern, as original wood had rotted away

A BORING TOOL
This drill or auger was used to make holes in planks, including rivet holes that held ship planking together. It had five bits of different sizes.

k gives extra strength

Tang, a spike that fits into a wooden handle

NE CUTTER
mall hacksaw could cut through
e and metal. The carpenter could
use its narrow blade for fine work.

WOOD SAW
The small lengths of wood needed to make buckets, boxes, and furniture were cut with this large saw.

Iron toothed blade

HAMMERS
Hammers came in various weights. The heaviest were used for welding and forging swords, the lightest for delicate work like shaping wire.

Small detachable bit

Larger detachable bit, for boring bigger holes

SHIP BUILDING
The Bayeux Tapestry (p. 10) shows how the Normans made ships. In the detail on the left, a man fells a tree. Above, a man trims a tree while another shapes the split trunks into planks with a T-shaped axe. Below, the planks are overlapped and riveted together. A carpenter smooths the planks. Another drills holes with a drill or auger, leaning against the curved end for extra force.

The carpenter turned this T-shaped handle to bore the hole

A smith's tools
The tools on these two pages are part of a large hoard found in a chest at Mästermyr on the island of Gotlánd, Sweden. Their owner was a smith. He was able to work with sheet metal to make cauldrons and locks, but he could also cast, weld, and decorate bronze. He was a ship-builder, joiner, and wheelwright, and probably made the wooden tool chest as well!

Shaped end for carpenter to lean on

Wooden handle

Spinning and weaving

VIKING WOMEN (and probably some men) spent part of the day spinning wool or flax. Then they wove the family's clothes on a vertical loom which stood against the wall. Everyday clothes were cut from plain wool. But the borders of men's tunics and women's dresses were woven with geometric patterns in bright colors or, for the very rich, gold and silver threads. Silk imported from far-off lands was made into hats and fancy borders for jackets. Fur trimmings on cloaks added a touch of style. Imitation fur was also fashionable.

Linen head cloth

Spindle whorl

SPINNING TOOLS
A spindle is a wooden rod used for spinning. It is passed through a spindle whorl, a round piece of clay or bone that makes the spindle spin with its weight. The weaver used rods called pin-beaters to straighten threads and make fine adjustments to the woven cloth.

Pin-beaters   Spind

Wool being stretched and spun

Raw wool

Medieval woman spinning with raw wool held on a distaff

Brown silk

Spun wool

SPINNING A GOOD YARN
The spinner picks a tuft of raw wool from the basket and pulls it into a strand. She winds this around the spindle as it spins. When one tuft is spun, she adds the next tuft of wool to the strand.

Spindle whorl

Spindle

Raw, combed wool

FANCY CLOTHES
Fragments of a chieftain's clothes were found a grave at Mammen, Denmark. They date fro the late 10th century. This is the end of a lon braid which the man may have used to fasten cloak. It is made of silk, with gold embroide on the borders. Animal figures and human fa also decorate the man's cloak and shirt. A reconstruction of his entire outfit can be seen page 29. The beautiful Mammen Axe (pp. 6– was found in the same grave.

Cane basket

WEAVING ON A VERTICAL LOOM

The warp (vertical threads) on a vertical loom are kept taut by weights at the bottom. There are two sets of warp threads, one on each side of the beam. The weaver passes the weft (a horizontal thread) between the two. Then she raises the heddle rod, which brings the back warp to the front, and passes the weft back again. After each pass she uses a weaving batten to push the new weft against the cloth above. Pass by pass, the woven cloth grows longer .

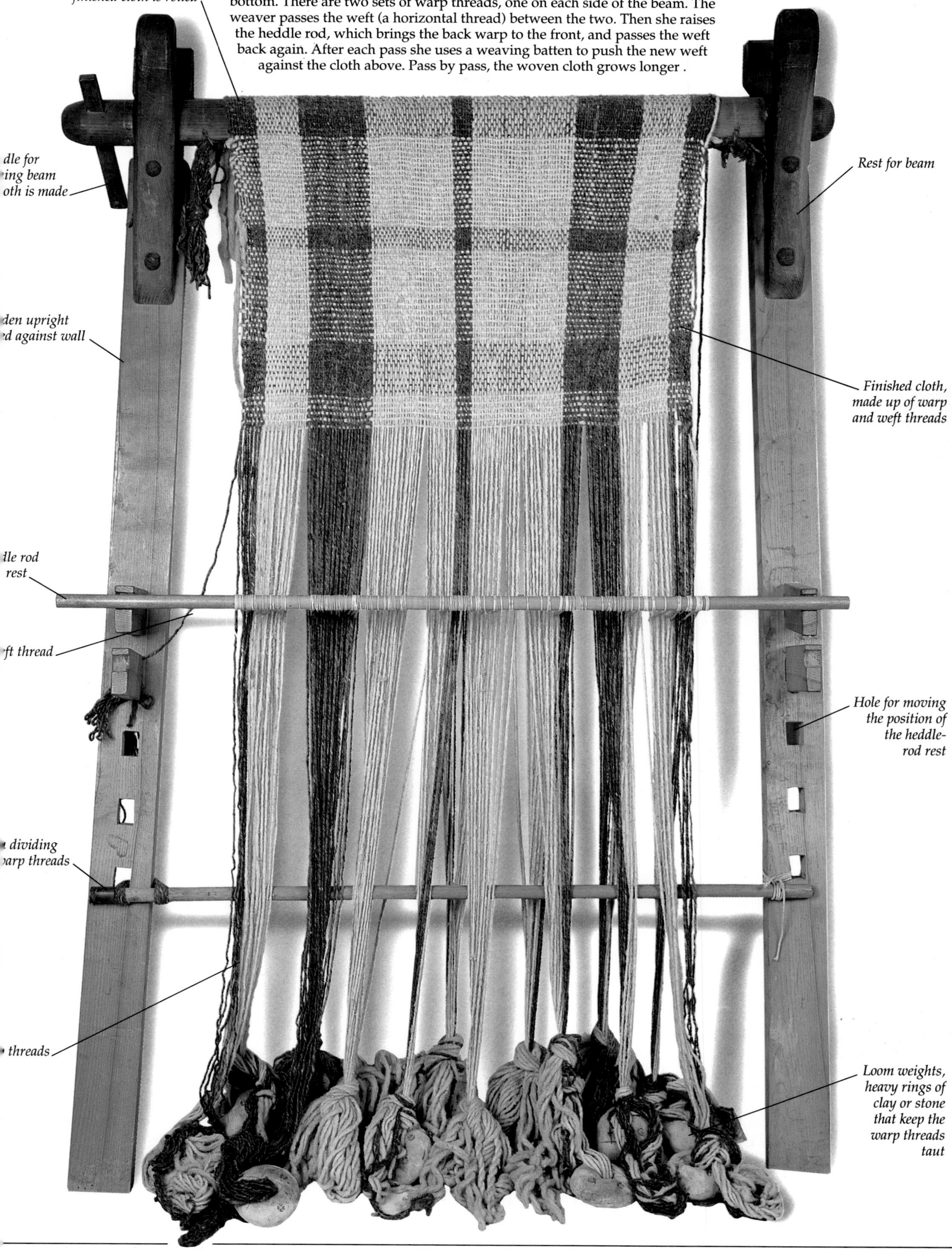

Cross beam where finished cloth is rolled

...dle for ...ing beam ...oth is made

...den upright ...d against wall

...dle rod ...rest

...ft thread

...dividing ...arp threads

...threads

Rest for beam

Finished cloth, made up of warp and weft threads

Hole for moving the position of the heddle-rod rest

Loom weights, heavy rings of clay or stone that keep the warp threads taut

Jewelry

GOLD PENDANT
Women wore pendants on the end of necklaces. This thin piece of embossed gold was worn as a pendant. It was found in a hoard (p. 49) in Halton Moor, England.

THE VIKINGS LOVED BRIGHT ornaments. Their metalworkers were highly skilled at the intricate decoration of jewelry. Both men and women wore brooches, necklaces, finger-rings, and arm-rings (like bracelets). Wearing gold and silver jewelry was a sign of wealth and prestige. After a successful raid, a king might reward a brave warrior by giving him a prize piece. Bronze didn't shine as brilliantly as gold, but it was less expensive. Pewter, a mixture of silver and other metals, was cheaper still. The poorest Vikings carved their own simple pins and fasteners from animal bones left over after cooking. Colored glass, jet, and amber were all made into pendants, beads, and finger-rings. Vikings also picked up fashions in jewelry from other countries and changed them to their own style.

Fine silver wires linked together as if they were knitted

SILVER ARM-RING
This massive arm-ring was found in Fyn in Denmark. It is solid silver, and must have weighed heavily on the arm. The surface is cut by deep, wavy grooves and punched with tiny rings and dotted lines. Four rows of beads decorate the center. They look as if they were added separately, but the whole piece was made in a mold (p. 42).

RECYCLING
Vikings who settled abroad took their styles with them. This gold arm-ring was made in Ireland. Vikings raided many Irish monasteries in search of precious metals. Sacred books and objects often had mounts made of gold and silver, which they ripped out and carried away. Later, smiths would melt the metals down and turn them into jewelry.

Animal heads

Gold wires of different thicknesses coiled together

SILVER SPIRAL
Spiral arm-rings could be worn high on the upper arm. They were only popular in Denmark, and were imported from the Volga area of Russia. This fine silver ring was found near Vejle in Jutland, Denmark.

Grooves are filled with niello, a black compound, to make them stand out

IN ALL HIS FINERY
This tough Viking is wearing every imaginable kind of jewelry. His bulging biceps are being squeezed by spiral arm-rings in the form of snakes. But in many details, the old drawing is pure fantasy (p. 6).

THOR'S HAMMER...
Thor's hammer (pp. 7, 53) was often worn as a pendant, just like the Christian cross. Here animal heads at the ends of the chain bite the ring from which the hammer hangs.

...AND A CROSS
An open, leafy patte[rn] decorates this silve[r] Christian cross. The c[ross] and chain were foun[d] Bonderup, Denmark. [They] were probably made a[round] the year 1050.

Four double-twisted gold rods braided together

Danish necklace
made of glass beads

NECKLACES AND RINGS
The Arab traveler Ibn Fadhlan (pp. 19, 55) met Viking women in Russia around 920. He wrote that "round the neck they have ornaments of gold or silver." These would have included neck-rings, which are stiff and inflexible, and necklaces, which can twist and bend. This gold neck-ring is the largest and most splendid ever found. It is solid gold and weighs over 4 lb (1.8 kg). It could only have been worn by a broad-chested man, because it is more than 1 ft (30 cm) wide! Many Viking neck-rings were made by melting down silver Arab coins. Glass made the brightest beads. Bead-makers started with imported glass or broken drinking glasses. They heated these up and fused them together to make beads with bright patterns and swirling mixtures of colors.

Silver neck-ring from
Halton Moor, England,
made of braided silver wires

armer in Tissø in
nmark found this
ssive gold neck-ring
le plowing a field

M-RING WITH TREES
s gold arm-ring from
ylille in Denmark is
nped with some very
decoration.

Cross

Gold ring from
Denmark inscribed
with runes (pp. 58–59)

Two gold finger-
rings from Viking-
age Ireland

THREE GOLD RINGS
Finger-rings were made like miniature arm-rings. Both men and women wore them. But Swedish women were the only ones to wear ear-rings, which they dangled from chains looped over the ear.

Continued on next page

Brooches

Clasps and brooches were often lavishly decorated. But they weren't just for show. All Vikings wore brooches to hold their clothes in place. Women usually had two oval brooches to fasten their overdresses (pp. 30–31). Men held their cloaks together with a single brooch on the right shoulder (pp. 28–29). In this way the right arm – the sword arm – was always free. Certain styles such as oval and trefoil brooches were popular all over the Viking world. Others, like the box brooches from Gotland, were only fashionable in certain areas.

Heads covered in gold

Hair

Beard

Long mustache

One of four squatting human figures made of gold

Ears

Side view of bronze box brooch from Gotland

Tin-coated ring and pin

BOX BROOCH
Box brooches were shaped like drums. The magnificent brooch on the left comes from Mårtens on the island of Gotland, Sweden. A very wealthy woman wore it to fasten her cloak. The base is made of cast bronze, but the surface glitters with gold and silver.

MEN'S HEADS
The tips of this broo[ch] from Høm in Denm[ark] are decorated with [the] men's heads. Each f[ace] has staring eyes, a n[ose] beard, and a long mustache. Brooches [like] this were first made [in] the British Isles. The Vikings liked them [so] much they made their own.

Head of slender animal

Top view of Mårtens box brooch, above

Head of gripping beast

Front view

Back view

SHAPED LIKE CLOVER LEAVES
Trefoil brooches have three lobes. In the 9th and 10th centuries, women wore them to fasten their shawls. The finest ones were made of highly decorated gold and silver. Poorer women had simpler brooches, mass-produced in bronze or pewter. The trefoil style was borrowed from the Carolingian Empire to the south of Scandinavia, in what is now France and Germany.

GRIPPING BEASTS
Four gripping beasts (p. 39) writhe across this silver brooch made in Hunderup in Denmark. It was found at the site of Nonnebakken, one of the great Viking forts (pp. 22–23).

URNES AGAIN
The Urnes art style featured a snak[e-like] animal twisting and turning in dyna[mic] coils (p. 38) It was the most popula[r] decoration for 11th-century brooches, [like] this bronze one from Roskilde, Denm[ark].

THE PITNEY BROOCH
The Urnes art style was very popular in England and Ireland during the reign of Cnut the Great (1016–35). This beautiful gold brooch in the Urnes style was found at Pitney in Somerset, England.

Long pin would have been stuck through cloak

Bronze pin, possibly from a brooch, in Irish style but found in Norway

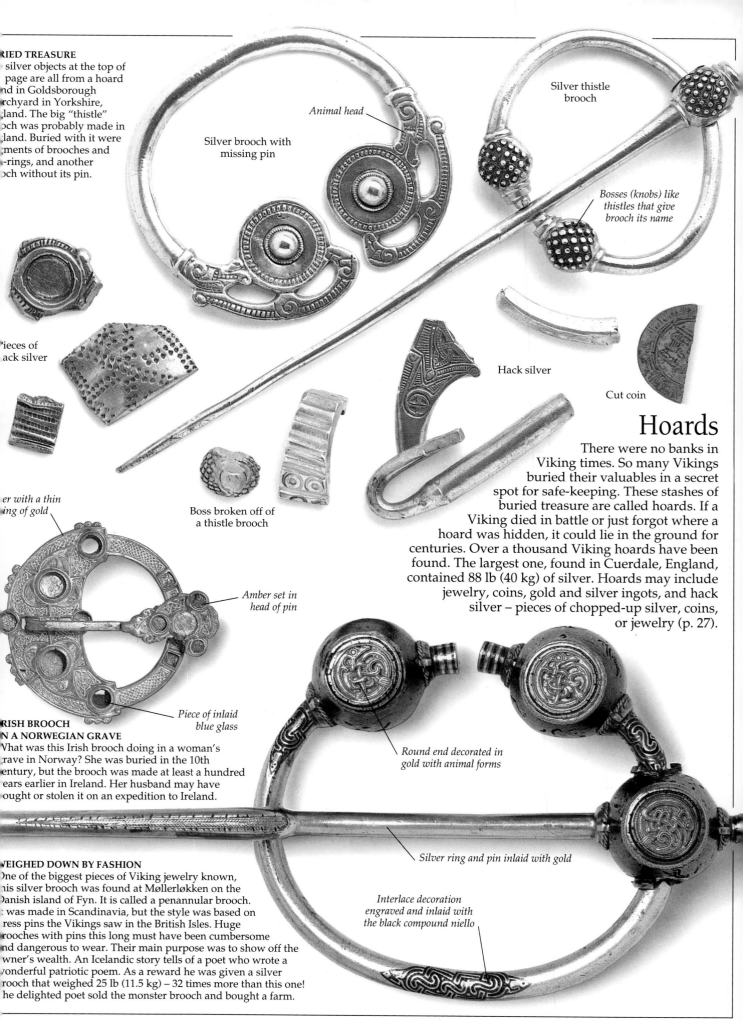

silver objects at the top of
page are all from a hoard
nd in Goldsborough
rchyard in Yorkshire,
land. The big "thistle"
och was probably made in
land. Buried with it were
ments of brooches and
-rings, and another
och without its pin.

Animal head

Silver brooch with
missing pin

Silver thistle
brooch

*Bosses (knobs) like
thistles that give
brooch its name*

Pieces of
ack silver

Hack silver

Cut coin

er with a thin
ing of gold

Boss broken off of
a thistle brooch

Hoards

There were no banks in
Viking times. So many Vikings
buried their valuables in a secret
spot for safe-keeping. These stashes of
buried treasure are called hoards. If a
Viking died in battle or just forgot where a
hoard was hidden, it could lie in the ground for
centuries. Over a thousand Viking hoards have been
found. The largest one, found in Cuerdale, England,
contained 88 lb (40 kg) of silver. Hoards may include
jewelry, coins, gold and silver ingots, and hack
silver – pieces of chopped-up silver, coins,
or jewelry (p. 27).

*Amber set in
head of pin*

*Piece of inlaid
blue glass*

RISH BROOCH
N A NORWEGIAN GRAVE
Vhat was this Irish brooch doing in a woman's
rave in Norway? She was buried in the 10th
entury, but the brooch was made at least a hundred
ears earlier in Ireland. Her husband may have
ought or stolen it on an expedition to Ireland.

*Round end decorated in
gold with animal forms*

Silver ring and pin inlaid with gold

WEIGHED DOWN BY FASHION
One of the biggest pieces of Viking jewelry known,
his silver brooch was found at Møllerløkken on the
Danish island of Fyn. It is called a penannular brooch.
: was made in Scandinavia, but the style was based on
ress pins the Vikings saw in the British Isles. Huge
rooches with pins this long must have been cumbersome
nd dangerous to wear. Their main purpose was to show off the
wner's wealth. An Icelandic story tells of a poet who wrote a
vonderful patriotic poem. As a reward he was given a silver
rooch that weighed 25 lb (11.5 kg) – 32 times more than this one!
he delighted poet sold the monster brooch and bought a farm.

*Interlace decoration
engraved and inlaid with
the black compound niello*

Games, music, and stories

A FEAST WAS A TIME to relax. After they had eaten their fill, Vikings played games, told stories, and listened to music. Kings had their own poets, called scalds, who entertained guests and praised the king. Stories and poems were told from memory and passed down from father to son. People knew all the exciting episodes by heart. Popular legends like Thor's fishing trip were carved on stone or wood (pp. 58–59). Jesters and jugglers often amused the guests with tricks and funny dances. Some games were played on elaborate boards with beautifully carved pieces. Others were scratched on wood or stone. Broken pieces of pottery or scraps of bone could be used as counters. Many outdoor pastimes were the same as today. During the long winters, Vikings went skiing, sledding, and skating (p. 40). In the summer, they fished, swam, and went boating in the cold rivers and fjords.

HORSE FIGHTING
These Icelandic ponies are fighting in the wild. Vikings enjoyed setting up fights between prize stallions (male horses). It was a serious matter, with bets laid on the winner. Horse-fighting may have played a part in religious feasts and ceremonies. The Vikings may have thought the winning horse was a special favorite of the gods.

SWEET HARP
In rich households, musicians played the harp or lyre to accompany stories and poems. Vikings were also keen singers. Talented singers would perform at feasts, and the whole assembly might join in a ballad or a popular folk song.

Such a headdress may have started the myth about Vikings wearing horned helmets

Sound is produced as air passes this hole

Blow here

BONE FLUTE
A Swedish Viking made this flute by cutting holes in a sheep's leg bone. He or she played it like a recorder, by blowing through one end. Covering the finger holes produced different notes.

Stave

Sword

Fingers cover bottom holes

Carved human head

Carved border decoration in Borre art style

Game pieces fit in 49 holes in board

BALLINDERRY BOARD
A popular Viking board game was *hneftafl*. One player used his eight pieces to protect the king from the other player, who had 16 pieces. This wooden board from Ballinderry, Ireland may have been used for *hneftafl*. The central hole could have held the king.

DANCING GOD
This silver figure from Sweden may be a "dancing god." He is carrying a sword in one hand and a stave or spear in the other. Dancing was popular after feasts, and played a part in religious ceremonies. Some dances were slow and graceful. In the wilder ones, the dancers leapt about violently. After the coming of Christianity (pp. 62–63), priests tried to stop dancing altogether.

FIGURES OF FUN
Gaming pieces could be simple counters or little human figures. This amber man (far right) may have been the king in a game of *hneftafl*. He is holding his beard in both hands.

Two walrus ivory gaming pieces from Greenland

Amber gaming piece from Roholte, Denmark

Hands hold beard

Another part of the story,
Sigurd's brother-in-law
Gunnar tries to escape
from a snake pit by
playing a lyre
with his toes
and charming
the snakes

Doorway was carved
around the year 1200

Fáfnir the
dragon

Sigurd kills
Regin

Sigurd
kills Fáfnir

DOOM OF THE GODS
The Vikings told stories of *Ragnarök*, the
"Doom of the Gods." This was a great
battle between good and evil, when the
gods would fight it out with horrible giants
and monsters. The detail above comes from
a 10th-century cross on the Isle of Man. It
shows the god Odin (pp. 52–53) being
eaten by the monstrous wolf Fenrir (p. 37).

Sigurd's horse Grani
loaded with treasure

Sigurd tests the
sword on the anvil
and breaks it in two

Birds in a tree

The story starts
with Regin forging
Sigurd's sword

Sigurd sucks his thumb
while cooking the
dragon's heart

SIGURD THE DRAGON-SLAYER
The adventures of the hero Sigurd are carved on
this wooden doorway from the church at
Hylestad, Norway. Sigurd won fame and fortune
by killing the dragon Fáfnir. The sword he used
was forged by the smith Regin, who was the
dragon's brother. But Regin was plotting to kill
Sigurd and steal the treasure for himself. Some
birds tried to warn Sigurd, but he couldn't
understand them. Luckily he burned his hand
cooking the dragon's heart and put his thumb into
his mouth. One taste of the dragon's blood and
Sigurd could understand the birds' twitterings.
So he grabbed his sword and killed Regin.

Gods and legends

THE VIKINGS BELIEVED IN MANY different gods and goddesses. The gods all had their own personalities, rather like human beings. The chief gods were Odin, Thor, and Frey. Odin, the go of wisdom and war, had many strange supernatural powers. Thor was more down-to-earth. He was incredibly strong, bu he wasn't very clever. Frey, a god of fertility, was generous The German traveler Adam of Bremen visited Uppsala i Sweden in 1075. He saw a great temple with statues of Odin, Thor, and Frey. Earlier in the Viking Age, peopl worshipped outdoors, in woods or mountains or by springs or waterfalls.

Cone-shaped hat

One hand holding beard, a symbol of growth

THREE GODS?
These three figures have been identified as Odin (l Thor (middle), and Frey (right). But they may b kings or Christian saints. They are on a 12th-century tapestry from Skog church in Sweden (p. 63).

GODLY FAMILY
Frey was a god of fertility and birth. The best image of him is this small statue from Södermanland in Sweden. It is only 2.8 in (7 cm) high. People called on Frey in the spring for rich crops. When they got married, they asked Frey to bless them and give them many children. His sister Freyja was a goddess of fertility and love. One story says that half the warriors killed in battle went to join Freyja, while the rest went to Odin.

MONSTROUS MASK
Frightening faces were sometimes drawn on memorial stones or pieces of jewelry (p. 7). They may be gods, or they might have been meant to scare off evil spirits. This face from a stone in Århus, Denmark, has a long braided beard and glaring eyes.

HIS LIPS ARE SEALED

Loki was part god and part devil. He could change his shape, and was always getting into mischief. In one story, Loki made a bet with a dwarf that he was a better metalworker. While the dwarf was heating up the furnace with bellows, Loki tried to distract him by turning into a fly and stinging him. But the dwarf won the bet anyway. To punish Loki and keep him quiet, he sewed his lips together. This stone bellows-shield shows Loki with his lips sewn up.

Silver Thor's hammer from Denmark

THOR'S HAMMER

Thor was popular with peasants and farmers. He rode through the sky in a chariot pulled by goats. There are many stories of his battles against evil giants and monsters, which he clubbed to death with his mighty hammer (p. 7).

A GIANT TAKES A BRIDE

In one story, the giant Thrym stole Thor's hammer. He said he would only give it back if he could marry Freyja. So Thor dressed up as Freyja and went to the ceremony. He nearly gave himself away by drinking too much! When Thrym brought out the hammer to bless the bride, Thor grabbed it and killed him and all the giant guests.

ERO'S WELCOME

Valkyries were warrior women who searched battle-
s for dead heroes. They carried warriors who had
bravely to Valhalla, the Viking heaven. Here Odin
comed the dead heroes, joining them in feasts in the
t hall every evening.

Dead warrior

ved roof of Valhalla

yrie (left) and
with axe (right)

yrie with
king horn
's dead hero

ic inscription

and rigging

PICTURES
OF VALHALLA

A hero arrives in Valhalla on this picture stone from Gotland (p. 58). He is riding Odin's eight-legged horse, Sleipnir. A Valkyrie holds up a drinking horn to welcome him. Under the curved roof of Valhalla, another Valkyrie gives a drinking horn to a man with an axe and a dog.

Ship full of armed warriors

Hero riding the eight-legged horse Sleipnir arrives in Valhalla

WATERFALL OF THE GODS

In Iceland, gods were worshipped at Godafoss, which means "waterfall of the gods."

TEARS OF GOLD

Freyja married a god called Od, who left her. All the tears she wept for him turned to gold. In this romantic picture, she is searching the sky for him in a chariot pulled by cats.

Viking burials

Before the coming of Christianity, Vikings were buried with everything they thought they would need in the afterworld. Funeral ceremonies varied a lot, and much is still shrouded in mystery. The wealthiest men and women were buried in ships, to carry them to the next world. These were crammed full of their belongings, from clothes and weapons to kitchen goods and furniture. Horses, dogs, even servants were killed and laid to rest with the dead Viking. The ships were then covered with mounds of earth, or set alight in a blazing funeral pyre. There are stories about burning ships being pushed out to sea, although there is no proof that this ever really happened. Other Vikings were placed in underground chambers in burial mounds. Even poor peasants were buried with their favorite sword or brooch.

Prow ends in snake's head

Intricate carvings of lively animals

BAGGY TROUSER
Three acrobatic hun figures are carved inside the prow of Oseberg ship. The have long, wispy beards and are doi strange gymnastic in baggy trousers

BURIAL MOUND
Amazing riches have been dug out of some burial mounds. Entire ships have survived in the right soil conditions. Even when the wood has disintegrated, the ship's outlines may be left in the earth. A ship from a mound in Ladby on Fyn, Denmark, has been traced in this way. Many mounds contain burial chambers, not ships.

Strakes get narrower toward the prow

Twelve strake each overlappi the one belo

Stem is a single piece of oak, joined to keel at

THE OSEBERG SHIP
The most beautiful Viking ship of all the Oseberg ship. It was discovered in 1903 in a burial mound in Oseberg near t Oslo Fjord in Norway. Like the Gokstad shi (pp. 8–9), it had been preserved by the soggy b clay of the fjord, or inlet. This is a modern copy of fine oak prow. Only fragments of the original were le in the mound. Like the sternpost, the prow is carved wit brilliant array of animals and people. It ends in a curling sna head, and the tip of the stern is the snake's tail. The ship is 70 ft 6 (21.5 m) long and has 15 oar-ports (holes) on each side. As many as 30 men were needed to row it. But the Oseberg ship is a frail vessel that could have sailed the open ocean. It was probably only used for state occasions o sailing up and down the coast. A mass of ship's equipment, including a gangplank, bailing bucket, mast, rudder, steering oar, anchor, and 15 pairs of oars, was found inside.

BUILDING THE OSEBERG SHIP

[Th]e Oseberg burial mound was 144 ft (44 m) long and 20 ft [(6 m)] high. It was excavated in the summer of 1904. The [shi]p inside was in bad condition. It had been filled with [he]avy stones, which had broken the wood into thousands [of] fragments. Each fragment was numbered, washed, [an]d protected with preservatives. Then the ship [wa]s put back together, piece by piece.

Prow, a snake's head in a spiral

Mast

Sternpost

Bailing bucket

Pine shield rack

Oars

Oar-ports

Hull of ship is made of oak

Keel, nearly 65 ft 8 in (20 m) long, made of two pieces of oak

INSIDE THE BURIAL SHIP

The Oseberg ship is the most sumptuous relic of a Viking burial. The bones of two women were found inside. They had been buried in the mid 9th century. Judging by the rich furnishings, one was probably a queen. The other may have been her slave or servant. The dead women must have once lain on the beds found in the burial chamber. These were littered with down and other remains of bedding. Two oxen and at least 10 horses had been slaughtered and thrown into the ship. Inside as well were a richly carved wooden wagon, three beautiful sleighs (p. 40), a work-sleigh, and many pieces of furniture, tapestries, and kitchenware such as an iron cooking cauldron (p. 35). The carving on some of these objects is superb.

WE BURN HIM IN A MOMENT

This is a re-enactment of a Viking funeral pyre. The Arab chronicler Ibn Fadhlan (pp. 19, 47) saw a Viking chieftain's funeral in Russia in 922. The dead man was dressed in beautiful clothes and seated in the ship, surrounded by drinks, food, and weapons. Then various animals and finally a woman were killed and laid in the ship with him. Then the ship was set on fire. Ibn Fadhlan was told: "We burn him in a moment and he goes at once to paradise."

BURIED BROOCH

No jewelry was found in the Oseberg ship, because the mound had been robbed long ago. But this bronze brooch was found in a woman's grave nearby. It is in the shape of an exotic animal with an arched head. The style is very similar to some of the Oseberg wood carvings.

[B]URIAL CHEST

[T]he burial chamber [o]f the Oseberg ship [c]ontained the fragments [o]f many wooden chests. [T]his is the most well [p]reserved one. It is made [o]f oak wood decorated [w]ith broad iron bands. [T]he elaborate locking [s]ystem includes three [i]ron rods that end in [a]nimal heads. The chest [w]as full of tools, which [t]he dead woman may [h]ave needed to repair [h]er vehicles in [t]he next world.

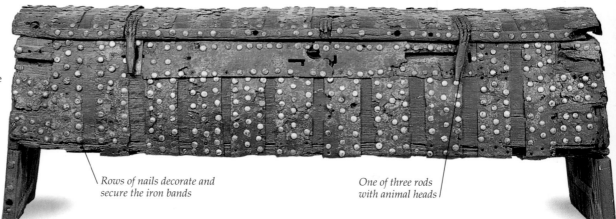

Rows of nails decorate and secure the iron bands

One of three rods with animal heads

Continued on next page

Whole mount is shaped like an animal's head and neck

Buried treasure

Vikings were buried with all kinds of treasures. These are known as grave goods. They are usually the finest or favorite belongings the dead man or woman owned or wore. Other grave goods were specially made, just to be buried. Grave goods give many glimpses of Viking life, of how people cooked or sewed, of their furniture, dress, and jewelry, and of the tools and weapons they used every day.

Head of person or animal

Paw

Face of animal, perhaps a lion

Tangle of legs

Two animal heads in profile, staring snout to snout

Eye

Long neck

Slender, S-shaped animal

Back leg

Front leg

Bird

BEAUTIFUL BRIDLE BITS
These five glittering pieces are part of a horse's bridle from the late 8th century. They were found with 17 others in a rich man's grave in Broa in Gotland, Sweden. Made of bronze and coated with gold, they are decorated with masses of intricate animals and birds, some twisting in slender ribbons, others plump and gripping everything in sight (p. 37).

Cast bronze handle

Spiral patterns engraved on bronze sheets

Clenched ja

Fe

Surface seethes with four-legged gripping beasts

The so-called "Carolingian" animal-head post

Mysterious head

Among the treasures in the Oseberg ship-burial were five strange wooden posts. Here a three of them. Each post is carved in a different style, but they are all topped by fantasti creatures with snarling mouth The carvers were incredibly skilled. The animals' heads ar necks squirm with a mass of tiny figures. No one knows w the posts were for. Worshippe might have carried them at a religious procession, perhaps the Oseberg funeral. The fierc animals, like lions, may have been meant to scare off evil spirits.

DRINKS BUCKET
Made in northern England or Scotland, this bucket was buried in a woman's grave in Birka, Sweden, around 900. It is made of birch wood covered in sheets of bronze. The bucket was probably used for serving drinks.

THE ENGLISH WAY

In their homes in Scandinavia, the Vikings raised huge memorial stones to remember dead friends or relatives (pp. 58–59). These stood in public places, often far from the dead person's grave. But in their colonies in England, the Vikings adopted the native custom of gravestones. This fragment of a stone from Newgate is decorated with two animals, one devouring the other. Traces of red paint show that it was once brightly colored.

Head of first animal

Second animal swallowing the first

SHIPS IN STONE

Only the very rich could afford a real ship to carry them to the next world. Other Vikings had their graves marked with raised stones in the shape of a ship. These ship settings are common all over Scandinavia. This is one of a whole fleet of ships in the big graveyard at Lindholm Høje in Jutland, Denmark.

PLANTS AND ANIMALS

These twisting figures decorate an 11th-century English gravestone. Two animals with S-shaped bodies form a figure eight pattern. Plant leaves and shoots sprout from their snaking bodies.

Large glaring eyes

Swirling circles carved in very high relief

ng nostrils

Two elegant, intertwining animals

Metallic fangs and eyes

Surface decorated with hundreds of nails with heads shaped like flowers

Open jaw with large bared teeth

The "First Baroque" animal-head post

The "Academician's" animal-head post

All five posts had long wooden planks attached to their bases with wooden dowels, or pins

VIKING SOAP OPERA

This romantic painting shows the funeral pyre of Sigurd the dragon-slayer (pp. 51, 58) and Brynhild (p. 30). In the legend, Sigurd was in love with Brynhild. But he married another woman instead and tried to trick Brynhild into marrying his brother-in-law, Gunnar. Brynhild was so angry that she had Sigurd killed. Overcome with grief, she stabbed herself and joined Sigurd on his funeral pyre.

Runes and picture stones

Vikings celebrated bravery in battle and the glory of dead relatives by raising memorial stones. These were carved with pictures and writing in runic letters (runes), often inside an intricate border of snakes. Some stones were raised by people who wanted to show off their own achievements. Others tell of loved ones who died on far-off voyages. The stones were set up in public places where many people could stop and admire them. The unusual picture stones from the island of Gotland often have no runes. But they are crowded with lively scenes of gods, ships, and warriors.

Sigurd's horse

Bir

Sigurd sucks his thumb

Headless body of Regin

Sigurd kills dragon

Drago
Fáfnir

SIGURD THE DRAGON KIL
The complete legend of Sigurd (p. 5
carved on a great rock at Ramsun
Sweden. The carver has clev
fitted clues about all the episo
into the frame made of sna
He has also turned on
the serpents into
dragon Fá.

Warrior killed in ba

The eight-leg
horse Slei
carries C
through the

The large pie
limestone was ca
and painted i
8th cen

Interlace b

Headless b
of the k
two

A JUMBLE OF PICTURES
This picture stone from Ardre, Gotland, is a jumble of pictures. But several stories can be picked out. At the top, Odin's mysterious eight-legged horse, Sleipnir, carries the god across the sky. Below is a Viking ship, surrounded by episodes from the bloody story of Völund the blacksmith. He was taken prisoner by King Nidud. In revenge, Völund cut off the heads of both of the king's sons and made their skulls into cups. In the end, Völund escaped by forging a pair of wings and flying away. The small boat below the ship may be the god Thor fishing with the giant Hymir. According to the legend, Thor caught the World Serpent. But Hymir was so terrified that he cut the line.

Völund's
with his han
and

Ship full of warriors, with large rectangular sail

May be Thor and Hymir fishing from small boat

The bird may be Völund flying away

Two figures fishing

Wild
perh
wol

Many other pictures cannot be identified with certainty

Medieval calendar stave carved with 657 different symbols

Writing in runes

Runes were easy to carve in stone or wood, with straight or diagonal lines. The basic alphabet had 16 runes. Runes were still used in Scandinavia well into the Middle Ages. The calendar stave (staff) from Sweden (above) shows how they developed.

Runes begin: "Hart's horn…"

INSCRIBED ANTLER
Bills, accounts, even love messages were written in runes on sticks. Part of this deer's antler from Dublin, Ireland, has been flattened to make a space for an inscription.

Secret runes which have not been deciphered

SECRET RUNES FROM GREENLAND
This pine stick from c. 1000 has the runic alphabet on one side. The other two sides are carved with secret and magical runes. No one knows what they mean.

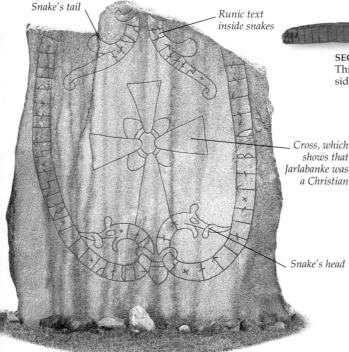

Snake's tail

Runic text inside snakes

Cross, which shows that Jarlabanke was a Christian

Snake's head

THORFAST'S COMB
Everyday objects were sometimes labeled in runes to declare their owner or maker. The runes on this comb case say: "Thorfast made a good comb."

F U TH A R K H N I A S T B M L R

FUTHARK
The basic runic alphabet was called *futhark*, after the first six letters. The first runic inscriptions, from around A.D. 200, are in a longer alphabet, with 24 characters. Around the year 800, the Viking alphabet with eight fewer runes was developed. Most inscriptions on stone were in normal runes. Another version of the alphabet was used for everyday messages on wood or bone.

SHOWING OFF
Jarlabanke was a wealthy 11th-century landowner who thought a lot of himself. He built a road over marshy land at Täby in Sweden. Then he raised four rune stones, two at each end, to remind travelers of his good deed. He also had this stone erected in the churchyard of Vallentuna, a village nearby. The runes say: "Jarlabanke had this stone raised in memory of himself in his lifetime, and made this Thing place, and alone owned the whole of this hundred." The "Thing place" was the spot where the assembly for the district met (p. 28–29). A Hundred was the area governed by a Thing.

SAINT PAUL'S STONE
In 1852, the end slab of a splendid tomb was found in the churchyard of St. Paul's Cathedral in London, England. The whole tomb must have been shaped like a box. This is a color painting of the great beast (p. 56) that decorates the slab. The colors are based on tiny traces of pigment found on the stone. The beast is very dynamic, twisting and turning around a smaller animal. The decoration shows that it was carved in the 11th century. The runes on the edge of the slab say: "Ginna and Toki had this stone set up." These two may have been warriors in Cnut the Great's army. Cnut became King of England in 1016 (p. 63).

The Jelling Stone

THE GREATEST STONE MONUMENT in Scandinavia is the Jelling Stone. It was raised by King Harald Bluetooth at the royal burial place of Jelling in Jutland, Denmark. Beside the stone are two huge mounds. One of these, the North Mound, may be where Harald's parents, King Gorm and Queen Thyre, were buried in a traditional ceremony (pp. 56–57). When Harald became a Christian, he built a church next to the mounds and had his parents re-buried inside. Then he raised the Jelling Stone in their memory. The memorial also advertised his own power as king of Norway and Denmark. This a modern copy of the stone. It is a three-sided pyramid, with a long inscription on one side and pictures on the other two.

SILVER MOUNT
King Gorm may have worn this mount on his belt. It was found in a grave in the church in Jelling, among the reburied bones of a man, probably Gorm.

Two entwir ribbon-l anim

GORM'S CUP?
This silver cup, usually known as the Jelling Cup, was found in the North Mound. It is the size of an egg. King Gorm may have drunk fruit wine from it. The cup is decorated with ribbon-like animals that gave their name to a style of Viking art, the Jellinge style.

Original stone is a single, massive boulder of red-veined granite

The great beast, a wild animal with sharp claws and a long tail

The beast is entwined in the coils of a huge snake

Ribbon-like decoration in Mammen style, a developm of the Jellinge style seen on cup, with the ribbons based plants rather than anim

Runes here continue from the inscription on the first side, reading: "…and Norway…"

GREAT BEA
One side of the st is carved with a sna twisting and turning aroun great animal. Their struggle represent the battle between g and evil. The animal could be a lion, it is often just called "the great bea It became a popular image in Viki art, and can be seen on weather vanes (p and rune stones like the St. Paul's Stone (p.

A ribbon forms a
border to the carving

Plant leaves and shoots spring
from the ends of the ribbon

...ese bright
...ors are only a
...ess, because the
...ginal pigment
... disappeared

...lo, a symbol of
...rist's holiness

...rist with
...stretched
...us

...vings are
...ow relief

Horizontal lines of
runes cut into stone

HARALD'S INSCRIPTION
One side of the Jelling Stone is covered in
runes (above). They read: "King Harald
commanded this memorial
to be made in memory of Gorm,
his father, and in memory of
Thyre, his mother – that Harald
who won the whole of Denmark
for himself, …" The inscription
continues beneath the great
beast (far left) and on
below Christ.

More plant-like
ribbons wrap
around Christ

Harald's inscription
ends beneath the
figure of Christ with:
"… and made the
Danes Christian."

...RDED
...RIST
... third side
...e stone is
...ed with the
...st picture of Christ
...candinavia. Christ's
... are outstretched, as if he
... on the cross, but no cross is
...ally shown. Harald was converted to
...istianity around 960. He was influenced
... miracle performed by the monk Poppo.
...he also converted for political reasons, to
...ngthen his kingdom and to make sure that
...mark could trade with Christian countries.

The coming of Christianity

SCANDINAVIA WAS SURROUNDED by Christian countries. Viking traders often wore crosses so they could travel freely through Christian lands (p. 27). But most Vikings remained loyal to the old gods until late in the 10th century. Then kings started supporting missionaries from England and Germany because they saw Christianity as a way to strengthen their power. Denmark converted to Christianity in the 960s, under King Harald Bluetooth. Norway followed early in the 11th century. In Sweden, the traditional beliefs survived until the end of the 11th century (p. 52). The Vikings finally gave the old gods up when they saw that kings or missionaries who destroyed their statues were not punished by Odin, Thor, or Frey.

RESURRECTION EGG
This colorful egg was a symbol of Christ's resurrection. It was made in Russia, and may have been brought to Sweden by Russian missionaries.

THE CHURCH AND THE SWORD
King Olaf Haraldsson turned Norway into a Christian country around 1024. He had old temples destroyed and forced people to convert.

STAVE CHURCH
Wooden churches were put up all over Scandinavia as soon as the people converted to Christianity. They were built like Viking houses, with wooden staves (planks) set upright in the ground. The first stave churches were simple, one-story buildings. By the 12th and 13th centuries, elaborate churches with many roofs were being built. This is the stave church from Gol in Norway, built around 1200, and now in the Folk Museum in Oslo.

Spire

Turret

Gables decorated with carved dragon heads like ones on reliquary, or shrine

More carved dragons

Portals are all crowned with crosses

Roofed-in veranda that runs all the way around church

LIKE A LITTLE CHURCH
Just like a miniature church, this little shrine or reliquary is decorated with dragon heads. Reliquaries were built to hold holy Christian relics. This one was made for Eriksberg church on Gotland, Sweden, in the late 1100s. Four little animal paws hold it up. The reliquary glitters with a thin layer of gold over its frame of carved wood. It probably once held bones or fragments of cloth that people believed came from the body or clothes of a saint.

BAPTIZED
aptism in water was a sign of
verting to Christianity. People
re the white baptismal clothes
or a week after the ceremony.

CHRIST THE TRIUMPHANT KING
The most powerful symbol of
Christianity is Christ on the cross.
Scandinavian artists interpreted
it in their own way. This crucifix
comes from Åby in Jutland,
Denmark. It is made of carved
oak covered in sheets of gilded
copper. Christ is shown as a king
wearing a crown. His eyes are
wide open, and only his hands
have nail holes. He looks
triumphant, not suffering.

Collar

CNUT THE GREAT
Born in Denmark, Cnut
invaded England in 1016.
By 1028, he was king of
Denmark, England, and
Norway. Though he took
England by the sword, he
was a Christian king who
built churches to make up
for the bloody raids of
his Viking ancestors.

*Hair hangs down
in long braids*

*Only hands are
nailed to cross*

Early Scandinavian
cross from Birka,
Sweden

*Knee-length tunic tied
in place with cords*

AWAY, DEVILS!
Ringing church bells to
call people to church was an
important way of shpwing
official Christianity. These
bell-ringers are woven on a
12th-century tapestry from
Skog church in Sweden
(p. 52). They are thought
to be ringing the bells to
keep the old gods away.

Cross

*Thor's
hammer*

Cross

BEST OF BOTH WORLDS
he old gods did not die
night. This stone mold from
nerland in Denmark shows
t craftsmen were happy to
ake Thor's hammers and
ian crosses at the same time.
Christian Vikings kept their
ith in Thor, just in case.

ADAM AND EVE
Scandinavian craftsmen
soon started depicting
scenes from the Bible as
well as dragons and
Viking legends. This
stone carving from Skara
church in Sweden shows
Adam and Eve being
expelled from Paradise.

Did you know?

FASCINATING FACTS

The Vikings came from all over the region that is now modern-day Scandinavia (Sweden, Norway, and Denmark). There was no unity between the Vikings: They fought one another as fiercely as they fought their enemies.

The word Viking may come from *vikingr*, meaning pirate, or from Viken, the area around the Oslo fjord in Norway; the same people were also called norsemen (men from the north) and even ashmen (from the wood they used to build their ships).

The Vikings' metalworking skills helped their society advance: The sharp axes they produced allowed them to cut down vast amounts of wood for building ships and constructing houses. On the land that was left clear, farmers could grow plentiful crops.

Ornamental axhead

In 1936, a Viking craftsman's chest was discovered in Sweden. It contained astoundingly modern-looking implements used for metalworking and carpentry, including tools fashioned in different sizes for fine and heavy work.

Because Vikings thrived under harsh conditions, their culture flourished, and coastal settlements became overcrowded. These conditions encouraged the first adventurers to set off in their ships to find new lands.

In parts of Sweden, many modern farms are still called Smiss ("the smith's farm") because traditionally, Viking farmers were also skilled craftsmen (smiths) who spent the winter traveling the countryside peddling their wares.

Viking farmers kept their livestock (mainly cows, sheep, and pigs) inside during the harsh winter months so that humans and animals could help keep each other warm.

Norwegian archaeologists have discovered a Viking house with an ingenious cavity-wall construction: a dry-stone outer skin, an inner lining of vertical planks, and a gap between them stuffed with grasses and moss for insulation.

Viking families often lit their homes with torches made from bundles of marsh grass called *lyssiv*, or light straw, which has a central core of wicklike white pith.

Vikings on Conquest, a watercolor by Johann Brandstetter

Early Viking raiders would arrive at a new land in the spring, spend the summer looting, then sail home for the winter.

When the marauders landed, locals would sometimes offer bribes in exchange for peace. In 911, the Normandy region of France was given to a Viking army in this way.

Viking ship by artist Christopher Rave

The first settlements made by Vikings in any new place were converted camps. Later, they brought in their families, built homes, and farmed the land, creating permanent communities.

Our word "Thursday" has its roots in Thor, the Viking god of thunder and lightning. Friday is named for Freya, wife of the most powerful god, Odin.

Viking swords were distinctively worked, with steel blades, iron guards, and pommels inlaid with silver, copper, and brass. Their basic design, however, was copied from weapons made in Rhineland (modern Germany) to the south.

Vikings prized their swords, and frequently gave them names such as Killer or Leg Biter. It was common practice for warriors to be buried with their weapons so they could use them in the afterlife.

Viking sword

Vikings despised weakness, even in children and babies. Sickly newborns who might be a burden on the family were often thrown into the sea or left outside to die.

Shakespeare's *Hamlet* was based on a character that first appeared in *Gesta Danorum*, a collection of ancient Viking tales. These were written down in the late 12th century by the Danish chronicler Saxo Grammaticus.

Because few people could read, it was the custom at the governing assembly for the Law Speaker to recite all the existing laws once a year.

QUESTIONS AND ANSWERS

Viking god Thor
in his chariot,
after a painting
by Max Koch

Q Do any of our important customs come from the Vikings?

A Our traditional Christmas celebration is largely rooted in Viking culture. Although many pagan societies enjoyed a midwinter festival, the Vikings actually exchanged presents at the winter solstice. In addition, they believed that their gods flew through the night sky carrying gifts in their chariots – an image uncannily like that of Father Christmas, or Santa Claus, in his airborne sleigh.

Q Was equality valued in Viking culture?

A Although Vikings kept slaves (mostly captured abroad), status in society was based as much on ability and acquired wealth as on noble parentage: although a son could inherit a lofty position from his father, a warrior of lowly birth could improve his social standing considerably just by acquiring wealth and impressive plunder on a series of foreign raids.

Q When Viking adventurers left their homes for months at a time, what kind of conditions did they live in?

A Although life at sea and in temporary camps was fairly primitive, it appears that the Vikings were not completely without comfort; from the burial site at Oseberg, archaeologists unearthed a large carved bed clearly designed to be taken apart and stored on board ships for use as camping equipment when the Vikings reached a new settlement.

RECORD BREAKERS

FIRST ARRIVALS
The first Europeans to colonize North America were Vikings, who landed in Newfoundland, Canada, in about 1001, nearly 500 years before Christopher Columbus made his famous journey.

FROSTY WELCOME
Vikings were also the first to settle in Iceland, arriving in 870. By 930, the fertile green coastal areas were densely populated.

BURIAL GROUND
The Viking cemetery in Lindholm Høje, Denmark, is one of the largest in the world, containing almost 700 graves, all marked with large stones.

PIONEERING TRADERS
The Vikings opened up many important international trade routes to places such as western Russia, the Mediterranean coast, northern India, and even the Middle East.

Q How religious were the Viking people?

A Faith was very important to the Vikings since it helped them to maintain their courage in a frightening world. In their mythology, for example, the souls of those who died from sickness or old age went to a shadowy, sinister domain, while warriors who died in combat would be taken to Valhalla to feast and engage in mock battles. Similarly, the Vikings considered the Norns – the Three Fates of Destiny – to be more powerful than gods and goddesses, a belief that may have made an extremely harsh existence easier to bear.

Q What role did women play in Viking society?

A Apart from the fact that most marriages were arranged by the couple's parents, women had a considerable amount of power and status. When their husbands were away on raids or explorations, they were left to run the farms, so they were capable and strong-willed. Once they were married, they could hold their own land. Until Vikings converted to Christianity, a wife was free to divorce her husband at will; if she left with the children, she was entitled to half her husband's wealth. A husband who left his wife was obliged to pay her compensation. Wives of chieftains and freemen (though not of slaves) were even allowed to contribute to political and legal debates.

Raw wool
ready for
spinning

Picture
stone from
Gotland,
Sweden

Who's who?

THE LEADING FIGURES in the Viking world tend to fall into one of three categories: rulers (at home and abroad), who held the power and made the laws; adventurers, who set off to find and colonize new lands; and writers and historians, who laid the groundwork for our knowledge of this remarkable civilization.

The king's memorial inscription to his parents in runes

King Harald Bluetooth's Jelling Stone

RULERS

• KING GUTHRUM
Danish ruler of East Anglia in the latter part of the ninth century. In 878, Guthrum signed the Treaty of Wedmore with Alfred the Great. This treaty divided England into two and made Guthrum overlord of the northern lands under Alfred's ultimate control. The area controlled by the Danes became known as Danelaw.

• ERIC BLOODAXE
King of Norway during the 930s, Eric was expelled for extreme cruelty: He is thought to have murdered his seven brothers. Eric Bloodaxe later became the last Viking ruler of Northumbria in England.

St. Olaf, patron saint of Norway

• KING HARALD BLUETOOTH
Ruler of Denmark during the 10th century, Harald Bluetooth converted his country to Christianity in the 960s. A great innovator, he commissioned the first bridge in Scandinavia and the biggest and most splendid of Viking memorial stones at Jelling in Jutland; Harald's parents, King Gorm and Queen Thyre, are thought to be buried at Jelling. Queen Alexandra, Danish wife of the 20th-century British king, Edward VII, is thought to have been descended from Harald Bluetooth.

• KING SVEIN FORKBEARD
Danish leader who besieged London in 994 until he was paid by King Ethelred II to withdraw; this payment was known as the Danegeld. In 1013, Svein Forkbeard returned, launching a successful invasion of England and seizing the throne. He died in 1014 and was succeeded by his son Cnut.

Gold brooch from the time of King Cnut

• KING CNUT (CANUTE)
Born in Denmark to Svein Forkbeard, the Christian king Cnut inherited his father's crowns in 1014, but was deposed in England by Saxon nobles who restored the previous king, Ethelred. When Ethelred died two years later, however, Cnut fought his son Edmund Ironside for the throne. Eventually Cnut and Edmund agreed to divide the country between them, but Edmund died soon after and Cnut became sole English king, as well as king of Denmark and, from 1028, of Norway. His reign was stable and prosperous, and he died in 1035, after which his empire collapsed.

• KING OLAF HARALDSSON
Ruler of Norway from 1015, Olaf II completed the process started by his predecessor, Olaf I, and made Norway a Christian country around 1024. He was killed in battle by his own chieftains backed by King Cnut of Denmark, and in 1164, he was declared his country's patron saint.

• KING HARALD HARDRADA
Harald III of Norway, known as Harald Hardrada, led a large Viking army that invaded Northumbria in England in September 1066. This army was defeated by the English king, Harold II, who was himself defeated by William the Conqueror at the Battle of Hastings in October of the same year.

• WILLIAM THE CONQUEROR
Leader of the Norman conquest of England in 1066, William was descended directly from Vikings who, under the chieftain Rollo, had settled in northwestern France during the first part of the 10th century.

William the Conqueror in a manuscript illustration

ADVENTURERS

Rollo, Duke of Normandy, portrayed in a Victorian print

- **BJORN JARNSMIDA**
Early Viking explorer who, with his companion Hasting, spent three years raiding lands far to the south of his homeland, such as Spain, North Africa, France, and Italy.

- **RAGNAR**
Viking chieftain who conquered Paris in 845. In order to reclaim the city, the French king, Charles the Bald, had to bribe Ragnar and his men with a large payment of silver.

- **ROLLO**
Ninth-century Viking chieftain who, with his followers, founded a settlement around present-day Rouen in France. As a result, this area became known as Normandy, or "land of the Northmen."

- **IVAR THE BONELESS**
Early Viking invader who landed in England in 869, conquering East Anglia and murdering its king, Edmund, when he refused to renounce Christianity. Edmund was later canonized, his shrine at Bury St. Edmunds becoming a place of pilgrimage.

- **ERIK THE RED**
Norwegian chieftain living in Iceland who, in 984, was accused of murder and banished. Setting off to discover new territory, he established a Norse settlement in Greenland in 986 and encouraged hundreds of Icelanders to settle there.

Rune stone carved by Viking settlers at Kingiktorsuak, Greenland

- **LEIF THE LUCKY (LEIF ERIKSSON)**
Viking explorer and son of Erik the Red, Leif is thought to be the first European to set foot in America, landing at the northern tip of present-day Newfoundland in Canada in about 1001. The Vikings called the new place Vinland (Land of Wine).

WRITERS AND HISTORIANS

- **IBN FADHLAN**
Tenth-century Arab writer who famously described the Vikings as "the filthiest of God's creatures." He also left fascinating descriptions of the precious jewelry worn by Viking women and the elaborate pyre he witnessed at the funeral of one of their chieftains.

One of Jarlebanke's four rune stones at the causeway he built in Täby, Sweden

- **SAXO GRAMMATICUS**
Danish chronicler and storyteller who lived between 1150 and 1206. One of the stories in his *Gesta Danorum*, a collection of traditional Scandinavian folk tales, is thought to have inspired *Hamlet*, William Shakespeare's play about a Danish prince.

- **JARLEBANKE**
Wealthy Swedish landowner and self-promoter who lived during the 11th century. The elaborate rune stones he erected in his own honor provide us with unique details about the region where he lived (called a Hundred) and the local assembly (or Thing) that governed it.

- **KING ALFRED THE GREAT**
An Anglo-Saxon king who defeated the Vikings in England, Alfred contributed greatly to our knowledge of Viking history by initiating the *Anglo-Saxon Chronicle*, a detailed history of England that covers the period of Viking invasion and domination.

Statue of Alfred the Great, located in his birthplace of Wantage, Oxfordshire

Find out more

MANY MUSEUMS WORLDWIDE have exhibits on Viking culture. The best ones, however, are usually found in the places where the Vikings lived and in the lands they conquered. Specialized museums of archaeology (the study of human antiquities) or anthropology (the study of people) are likely to have the most on display, and they may also have good libraries and bookstores with further information.

One such museum is the Roskilde Ship Museum in Denmark. Visitors can view five different ships that sank around the year 1000 and were excavated in 1962. There is also a nearby museum full of Viking documents and artifacts, and a research center with a re-created Iron-Age village, complete with gardens, workshops, and animals.

MODEL MUSEUM
Visitors to the Roskilde Ship Museum are encouraged to learn how the Vikings constructed their craft by watching scale models being made. Produced by skilled local boat builders, these models are authentic in almost every detail.

TRIPS IN TIME
In addition to scale models, full-sized replicas of Viking longships are built at Roskilde. During the summer months, they take visitors on both short sailing trips and extended excursions along old Viking routes.

ILLUMINATING THE PAST
Like many up-to-date visitor facilities, the separate cultural museum at Roskilde uses imaginative displays and models to bring the ancient world to life. Roskilde was the original capital of Denmark.

RINGS OF GOLD
Because the Vikings were so well traveled, many large museums have impressive displays of their artifacts and jewelry. These rare gold rings come from the British Museum in London.

Reconstructed Viking dwelling at L'Anse aux Meadows

VINLAND UNEARTHED
Although Vikings landed in Newfoundland, Canada, during the 11th century, it was not until the 1960s that the site of their settlement was discovered at a fishing village called L'Anse aux Meadows (the name is an anglicized version of the French *L'Anse a la Medée*, or Medea Bay). Like those in Iceland, these Viking houses had timber frames covered with layers of turf.

GODS AND LEGENDS
The images on this 11th-century picture stone illustrate ancient Norse legends about the god Odin and members of his family. The stone is in the Museum of National Antiquities in Stockholm.

TREASURES FROM ABROAD
Although this graceful glass vessel (in the collection of the Museum of National Antiquities in Stockholm) was found in a Viking grave in Scandinavia, it would originally have come from an area farther south, in present-day Germany.

USEFUL WEB SITES

- Visit the Vikings at the British Museum:
  www.bbc.history/ancient/Vikings
- Can't get to Denmark? Stop by the site for the Viking Ship Museum in Roskilde (click on English under the Languages menu if you don't speak Danish):
  www.vikingeskibsmuseet.dk
- Web site of the Vikings, a large re-enactment society with members in the United States and Europe:
  www.vikingsna.org
- The site for the Borg Viking Museum is full of Viking information:
  www.lofotr.no/engelsk/index.htm
- Explore a Viking village, discover the secrets of Norse ships, and write your name in runes:
  www.pbs.org/wgbh/nova/vikings
- The North Atlantic Saga online exhibit:
  www.mnh.si.edu/vikings/start.html

Places to visit

L'ANSE AUX MEADOWS, NEWFOUNDLAND, CANADA
A reconstruction of three buildings at the only authenticated Viking site in North America, which is also a UNESCO World Heritage Site. Visitors can see:
- details about the archaeological discovery of the settlement
- exhibits that link Viking artifacts found there with everyday Viking life.

VIKING SHIP MUSEUM, ROSKILDE, DENMARK
Located right in the harbor, this museum was built in 1969 specifically to display the ships discovered in the Roskilde Fjord. Of particular interest are:
- the displays that focus on the Vikings in Ireland, and the meeting of the two cultures
- the museum shop, which sells copies of Viking jewelry and domestic objects.

TRELLEBORG VIKING FORTRESS, WEST ZEALAND, DENMARK
An ancient ring fortress constructed about 980, Trelleborg is situated in beautiful countryside and includes among its attractions:
- a museum where items excavated at the site are displayed and exhibitions are mounted to provide information about the fortress and how it was used
- activities and shows – many of them interactive – that offer an intimate look at who the Vikings were and how they lived.

BORG VIKING MUSEUM, NORTHERN NORWAY
An accurate reconstruction of a Viking chieftain's homestead, this living museum is the result of years of archaeological excavation and research. On display are:
- objects and artifacts (many unearthed on the site) that demonstrate the connection between the Vikings and southern Europe
- a reconstructed Viking ship.

BRITISH MUSEUM, LONDON, ENGLAND
In both the Early Medieval and the Coins and Medals galleries, there are outstanding Viking collections, which include:
- the Cuerdale hoard of more than 8,500 objects, such as coins and hack silver
- the Goldsborough hoard, including a large thistle brooch
- a whalebone plaque adorned with horse-head images and used for smoothing linen.

JORVIK VIKING CENTRE, YORK, ENGLAND
Sitting on the site of the ongoing Coppergate Viking excavations, this museum attempts to re-create the sights, sounds, and smells of the Viking era. Its key features include:
- interactive rides where visitors are taken through re-created homes and businesses from the 10th century.
- an artifacts gallery that shows visitors what the objects looked like in Viking times and how they looked when they were first found by archaeologists.

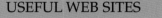

Pendant image of the goddess Freya, on display at the Stockholm antiquities museum

Glossary

ADZE A cutting tool with an arched blade

ANVIL (*see also* SMITH) Solid block (usually made of iron) on which metal is worked by a smith

ARD Basic plow that breaks up the earth with a pointed blade

AUGER Handled tool for boring holes in wood

BALDRIC Leather sword strap, usually worn diagonally across the body

BARBARIAN Coarse, wild, or uncultured person. Vikings were considered by many to be barbarians.

BOSS Projecting knob or stud

BOW (or PROW, *see also* STERN) Prow, or front section, of a ship

BYRE Rudimentary shed for cattle

CASKET Small box or chest, often ornamental, intended for valuables or religious relics

CAULDRON Large pot made from iron or stone. Vikings cooked in cauldrons set over a fire or suspended from a roof beam.

Cauldron

CAULKING (*see also* STRAKE) Material (often tarred wool or loose rope fibers) stuffed between the strakes of a ship to act as waterproofing

CHAIN MAIL Protective armour made from small interlaced iron rings

CLINKER (*see also* STRAKE) Boat-building technique in which each external strake overlaps the one below

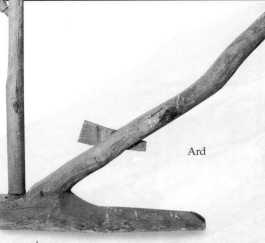

Ard

CRAMPONS Iron studs nailed to the hooves of Viking horses to prevent them from slipping on icy ground

CRUCIBLE Pot in which metal is melted

DAUB (*see also* WATTLE) Clay or dung plastered over wattle as waterproofing to form a wattle-and-daub wall, fence, or roof

DEMOCRACY System of government in which the people being governed have a voice, usually through elected representatives

DIE Engraved stamp used for making (also called striking) coins, medals, or brooches

FIGUREHEAD Ornamental carving (sometimes detachable) on the prow of a ship

FINIAL Decorative projection extending from the apex of a roof, gable, or pediment

FJORD Long narrow arm of ocean or sea stretching inland, often between high cliffs

FULLER Central groove cut into a sword's blade to make it lighter and more flexible

FUTHARK (*see also* RUNE) Scandinavian runic alphabet, named after its first six letters (the "th" sound counts as one letter)

GANGPLANK Movable plank used for walking on or off a boat

GUARD (*see also* HILT) Crosspiece between a sword's hilt and blade that protects the user's hand

GUNWALE (or GUNNEL) (*see also* STRAKE) Upper edge of ship's side; top strake

HACK SILVER Chopped up bits of jewelry and coins used as currency

HILT Handle of sword or dagger

HNEFTAFL Viking game played with counters on a wooden board

Piece of hack silver

HOARD Stash of buried Viking treasure, which may include jewelry, coins, and other items made from precious metal

HULL Body or frame of a ship

JARL (*see also* THRALL, KARL) Earl, noble or chieftain; one of the three classes in Viking society

KARL (*see also* THRALL, JARL) Free man (as opposed to slave); largest of the three classes in Viking society. Farmers, traders, craftsmen, warriors, and major landowners were all karls.

Viking longship

Ship's keel

KEEL Lengthwise timber along the base of a ship on which its framework is constructed

KEELSON Line of timber fastening a ship's floor timbers to its keel

LONGSHIP Ship powered by lines of rowers as well as a single rectangular sail

MAST Timber or iron pole that supports a ship's sails

MOOR To attach a ship to a fixed structure or object

NIELLO Black metallic compound of sulfur with silver, lead, or copper used for filling engraved lines in silver

OARPORT One of the holes in the side of a longship through which the oars project

ORTUGAR Viking unit of weight made up of three smaller units called ORE, and equal to about 0.25 oz (8 g)

PIN BEATER Slender wooden rod used in weaving to straighten threads and smooth the cloth

PROW (or BOW, *see also* STERN) Front section of a ship or boat

PURLIN Horizontal beam supporting the main rafters in a typical Viking house

QUERN Small round stone mill for grinding grain into flour

RAMPART Defensive mound of earth and turf supported by a wooden framework

RIGGING Arrangement of a ship's mast, sails, ropes, and related equipment

RUNES Early Scandinavian letters, many of which were formed by modifying Greek or Roman characters to make them suitable for use in carving

RUNE STONE Memorial stone carved with writing, pictures, and decorative motifs

SCALD Viking term for a composer and reciter of epic poems about kings and heroes

SCUTTLE The action of sinking a boat or ship deliberately

SHINGLES Thin, overlapping wooden tiles used for roofing on traditional Viking houses

SHROUD Set of ropes supporting the mast

SICKLE Handled implement with a curved blade used for harvesting grain or trimming growth

SLEDGE Flat surface on runners. Like Egyptian pyramid builders, Vikings used sledges to carry heavy loads. Richly decorated – perhaps ceremonial – examples have been discovered in burial hoards.

SMITH Metalworker, as a goldsmith or tinsmith. A blacksmith is someone who works in iron.

The 10th-century Jelling Stone with its memorial runes

SPELT Early variety of wheat, which produces particularly fine flour

SPINDLE Small rod with tapered ends used for twisting and winding the thread in spinning

SPINDLE WHORL Round piece of clay or bone attached to a spindle whose weight helps it to spin

STAVE Upright wooden plank, post, or log used in building construction

STAVE CHURCH Wooden church built like a Viking house, with wooden planks (staves) set upright in the ground. Stave churches were constructed across Scandinavia after the arrival of Christianity.

STERN (*see also* BOW OR PROW) Hind or rear section of a ship

STERNPOST Ornamental carving (sometimes detachable) on the stern of a ship

STRAKE Horizontal timber plank used in the construction of ships

TANG Metal projection on a blade or a bit, designed to fit into a wooden handle.

THING Local assembly. Every district was subject to the rule of its Thing, and all free men could express opinions there.

THRALL (*see also* KARL, JARL) Viking slave (man, woman, or child who is owned by another person in the same way as an item of property, usually to do work of some kind); one of the three classes in Viking society

TILLER Horizontal bar fitted to the top of a steering oar or rudder

Valkyrie pendant

TREFOIL Three-lobed motif that was popular in the design of Viking jewelry, particularly brooches

VALKYRIE Female warrior in Norse mythology.

WARP (*see also* WEFT) Lengthwise threads on woven cloth

WATTLE (*see also* DAUB) Interwoven branches used to form the basic structure of walls, fences, or roofs

WEFT (*see also* WARP) Crosswise threads on woven cloth; weft threads pass over and under the warp threads

Shroud

Mast

Viking longship

Tiller

Oarport

Hull

Index

Acknowledgments

The publisher would like to thank: Birthe L. Clausen at the Viking Ship Museum, Roskilde, Denmark; Vibe Ødegaard and Niels-Knud Liebgott at the National Museum of Denmark, Copenhagen; Brynhilde Svenningsson at the Vitenskapsmuseet, Univ. of Trondheim, Norway; Arne Emil Christensen and Sjur H. Oahl at the Viking Ship Museum, Oslo, Norway; Lena Thalin-Bergman and Jan Peder Lamm at the Statens Historika Museum, Stockholm, Sweden; Patrick Wallace and Wesley Graham at the National Museum of Ireland, Dublin; Elizabeth Hartley at York Museum; Christine McDonnel and Beverly Shaw at York Archaeological Trust, England; Dougal McGhee; Claude and Mimi Carez; Niels and Elizabeth Bidstrup in Copenhagen and Malinka Briones in Stockholm for their warm hospitality; Norse Film and Pageant Society; Helena Spiteri for editorial help; Manisha Patel and Sharon Spencer for design help.
Additional photography: Geoff Dann (models 12, 13, 19, 27, 28, 30, 31, 44 and animals 37, 38–39); Per E. Fredriksen (32bl, 32–33); Gabriel Hildebrandt at the Statens Historika Museum, Stockholm; Janet Murray at the British Museum, London.
Illustrations: Simone End, Andrew Nash
Index: Céline Carez
Picture credits:
(t=top b=bottom c=center m=middle l=left r= right)
Archeological & Heritage Picture Library, York: 16bc; AKG London: 64bl, 65tl, 67tl; Bibliothèque Nationale, Paris: 16br. Biofoto, Frederiksberg/ Johann Brandstetter 64c/ British Museum 66br/ Karsten Schnack: 20cl/ Jurgen Sorges 69tl/JK Winther: 22cr; Bridgeman Art Library, London: Jamestown-Yorktown Foundation/©M Holmes: 21tl, /Musée d'Art Moderne, Paris/Giraudon, Wassily Kandinsky "Song of the Volga" 1906, © ADAGP, Paris and DACS, London 1994: 19br, /Russian Museum, St Petersburg, © Ilya Glazunov "The Grandsons of Gostomysl": 18bl; British Museum: 2bc, 4cal, 5bc, 6cr, 14c, 16cl, 25tr, 27cl, 29bl, 29br, 30bl, 36bc, 37cl, 46tl, 46c, 47c 2nd out, 47br, 48bl, 49tr, 59cr 4th down, 70bc; Buster Ancient Farm: 70tc. Jean-Loup Charmet, Paris: 6tl, 10tl, 16c, 19tr, 34tl, 38br; Corbis: Ted Spiegel 68tr, 68cl, 68-69. Danish National Museum: 64cl. DAS Photo: 55cl; CM Dixon: 12br, 53cr, /Museum of Applied Arts, Oslo: 13tl; Mary Evans Picture Library: 14cr, 17tc, 20tl, 30tl, 46bc, 53cl, 53br; Fine Art Photographs: 57bl; Forhistorisk Museum, Moesgård: 52br; Werner Forman Archive: 21tr, 24br, 71tc /Arhus Kunstmuseum, Denmark: 53tl, /Statens Historiska Museum: 52cr, 63br, 65br, 66bl, 69c, 69bc. /Universitetets Oldsaksamling, Oslo: 43cl; Michael Holford/Musée de Bayeux: 10bl, 15cr, 34tr, 34br, 35bl, 38bl, 38bc, 43tr, 43cr; Frank Lane Picture Agency/W Wisniewski: 50tr; Mansell Collection: 12bl, 50tl; Museum of London: 44tc, 44cr; © Nasjonalgalleriet, Oslo 1993/J Lathion: Christian Krohg "Leiv Eiriksson discovering America" oil on canvas (313 x 470cm): 24tr, Johannes Flintoe "The Harbour at Skiringssal" oil on canvas (54 x 65 cm) (detail): 28bl; National Maritime Museum: 24cal, 70cr, 71b/James Stephenson: 25car, ; Nationalmuseet, Copenhagen/Kit Weiss: 29tr, 29c, 44br; National Museum of Ireland: 7cr, 16tr, 17tr, 50cr, 59tr 2nd down; Peter Newark's Historical Pictures: 11cl, 17cl; Novosti /Academy of Sciences, St Petersburg: 22tr; © Pierpont Morgan Library, New York 1993 M736 f 9v: 7bl, f 12v: 17tl; Mick Sharp: 38tr; Statens Historiska Museum, Stockholm / Bengt Lundberg: 28tl; TRIP: 32tr 57tl; Universitets Oldsaksamling, Oslo: 8tr, 9l, 13tr, 13cl, 25tc, 32cr, 43cl, 51cl, 55tl, 55tr, 55cr Vikingeskibs-hallen Roskilde/Werner Karrasch: 11tc; Williamson Collection: 70bl. Stockholm Vitenkapsmuseet, University of Trondheim/ Per Fredriksen: 30cl, 32bl, 32/33b; Eva Wilson: 59br.

Jacket credits
Front cover: Tl: Peter Anderson © Dorling Kindersley, Courtesy of the Universitets Oldsaksamling, Oslo, Norway; Tc: The National Museum of Denmark, Copenhagen, Denmark; Tr: British Museum, UK; B: Mandy Collins/Alamy. **Back cover:** DK Picture Library: Danish National Museum br, c, cb; Viking Ship Museum, Norway bc, t, bl, tl.

All other images © Dorling Kindersley. For more information see:
www.dkimages.com